The Town of Hercules

The Town of Hercules

A buried treasure-trove

Joseph Jay Deiss

Evans Brothers Limited   London

First published in Great Britain 1976 by Evans Brothers Limited,
Montague House, Russell Square, London, WC1 5BX
Original edition first published 1974 by Houghton Mifflin Company,
2 Park Street, Boston, Mass. 02107

© Joseph Jay Deiss 1974

Set in 12 on 13 point Baskerville and printed in Great Britain by
Hazell Watson & Viney Ltd, Aylesbury, Bucks

ISBN 0 237 44838 6   PRA 4818

Contents

Acknowledgements

We are grateful to the following sources for permission to include photographs in this book: Alinari, Naples, photographs on pages 44, 52, 68, 101, 102, 123, 131; Vincenzo Carcavallo, Naples, photographs on pages 8, 37, 61, 74, 76, 77, 78, 100; E.N.I.T. (Italian State Tourist Office), New York, photograph on page 27; Johannes Felbermeyer, Rome, photographs on pages 13, 16, 47, 53, 58, 62, 82, 86, 115, 124, 132; Fotocielo, Rome, photograph on page 40; Fototeca Unione, Rome, photographs on pages 45, 50, 66; S. Giordano, Naples, photograph on page 19; Superintendent of Antiquities, Naples, photographs on pages 14, 15, 16, 18, 32, 41, 42, 46, 47, 55, 56, 57, 58, 59, 60, 65, 67, 68, 70, 82, 83, 85, 87, 89, 90, 91, 97, 103, 104, 105, 108, 109, 113, 117, 118, 121, 124, 129, 132, 133, 134, 135; the Getty Art Museum photographs on pages 31, 73.

Introduction

Each year thousands of people visit the many historical sites of Britain. They wander around castle walls, through abbey ruins and over ancient earthworks. They cross fields on foot to examine standing stones or park the car right outside a local museum.

Why are so many people attracted to these old remains? Many of the visitors are students who are examining the site as part of their work. You may have been on a school expedition like this. Some are holiday-makers or day-trippers who are filling in a spare half-hour. But mostly they are people who are interested in old things and who hope there will be something worthwhile to see.

If you have walked along the castle walls at Harlech, stood beneath the huge upright stones at Stonehenge, or climbed the steep ramparts of Maiden Castle you may have experienced some wonder and excitement which made the visit worthwhile.

The trouble with many historical sites is that they may not, at first, appear very exciting. Often all that remains are a few low walls neatly surrounded by grass. If you are lucky there may be a museum on the site. Here you can sometimes buy a guide and look at things which have been found.

But bits of broken pot, a few coins or bones and some fragments of metal don't tell you much, and the official guide may be written in a way you can't understand. If you are fortunate, you may buy a postcard showing an artist's reconstruction of how the place perhaps once looked. This can help you visualise the buildings more easily because it includes the bits that have long since disappeared.

Another problem is discovering what the people were like who defended the site, or lived and worked there. Many visitors must come away disappointed. They had expected to see much more, and they are left with many unanswered questions.

Undoubtedly there are some marvellous historical places in Britain, with good museums and guides specially written for children. But there is not a Roman site like the one which this book describes. The town of Herculaneum, as you will discover, is unique because there is so much to see and, because so much still remains, a very accurate picture can be built up of how the inhabitants lived and who they were.

OLIVER ASTON

Central cone of Mount Vesuvius during the mild eruption of 1943. The photograph was taken with a telescopic lens. Stones the size of footballs were hurled for many miles, amid volcanic "grunts" and roars.

1 The mountain called Vesuvius

It is difficult for most of us to imagine living at the foot of an active volcano. Those who do seem to think nothing of it.

Near the city of Naples, in southern Italy, thousands of people now live on the slopes of Mt. Vesuvius. Some of them occupy the simple one-storey stone houses of their peasant ancestors. Many more occupy modern ten- or twelve-storey reinforced concrete blocks of flats. These people will tell you that they are not in the least afraid of the volcano. Yet everyone knows that neither the old nor the new buildings are safe.

High on the volcano is a watchtower. There scientists are on guard day and night. The scientists measure every movement and take the volcano's temperature at regular intervals. Lack of smoke and steam may indicate that internal pressure is rising. When the temperature goes up, warning alerts are issued.

The people say that they know the habits of "Vesuvio." They say that "he" always gives warning before one of "his" periodic eruptions. They tell tales of various eruptions and say that volcanic "grunts" are danger signals. Everyone believes that in case of a new eruption there will be time to run away.

The truth is that volcanoes are not dependable. Very little accurate information about them exists. They date from when the earth was young, but only in recent years has any effort been made to find out what they are really like.

More dangerous than living at the foot of an active volcano is living near a volcano that is thought to be spent, but actually is not dead. Then the eruption can come without warning — often as a gigantic explosion — and so cause a major disaster.

That is what happened to the people who were living on the slopes of Mt. Vesuvius in the year we call A.D. 79. Most thought that Vesuvius was an ordinary mountain. Only a few thought it was a dead volcano. Many little towns were spread beneath it along the shore of the Bay of Naples. Today we know the details of only two: Pompeii and Herculaneum. These are the only two that have been even partially cleared of the volcanic matter that covered them.

The process of digging up an ancient site is called an "archaeological excavation" — because the word *archaeology* itself means the scientific study of ancient peoples. It has come into the English language from Greek words. Sometimes archaeologists refer to an excavation as a "dig."

Herculaneum was discovered before Pompeii, but it is less famous than Pompeii. It proved much more difficult than Pompeii to uncover. This book is the story of Herculaneum — the town of the hero-god Hercules. It is pronounced *Her-cu-lă-neum* in Latin, the language of the people who lived there at the time of the great eruption. In the language of the people who live there now, the Italians, it is pronounced *Er-co-lă-no*.

In many ways Herculaneum is more interesting than Pompeii because it is better preserved. A visit now is almost like a visit to the living town of two thousand years ago.

Perhaps some of the readers of this book will go to Italy some day and see Ercolano for themselves.

2 A busy morning in the town of Hercules

Young Romans — like their elders — woke up at sunrise to make the most of the day's light. In Herculaneum, sunrise on August 24 in the year A.D. 79 seemed no different from any other dawn on a hot morning. Babies cried. Older children and adults yawned, rubbed their eyes, and rolled out of bed as usual.

The Bay of Naples was blue and glassy calm. The mountain called Vesuvius was green with olive trees and vineyards. The sky was free of clouds and the sun was brilliant. It was a perfect day for swimming, boating, playing games, or rambling in the country.

The boys and girls of Herculaneum washed their faces in the cool water that flowed from the mountains in man-made channels called aqueducts. They put on their simple clothes, tied their sandals, combed their hair. Wild birds sang, and birds in cages answered. Lizards flicked long tongues at buzzing flies. Insects rasped in the tall dark cypress trees. Here and there a donkey brayed and a horse whinnied. The fishermen, who had put to sea before dawn's light, were already bringing their boats with sails of many colours back to shore. They had a good catch.

It was to be a busy morning in Herculaneum for everybody. First breakfast, with fresh fruit, cereal or bread and honey, milk or a little wine. Then teeth were cleaned. Some people went off to work, housewives turned to their chores, and young Romans occupied themselves according to their age and class.

In August there was no school, so the younger children were free to run and play. Teenage boys worked as apprentices learning trades. Girls worked at looms or helped their mothers by tending younger brothers and sisters. Sons of wealthy families were expected to study for a few hours under tutors, for education was considered very important. Boys of all ages were active in athletic events.

The town of Hercules was in one of its gayest moods because a festival was in progress. It was the celebration of the official birthday of the Emperor Augustus, who had been dead for sixty-five years. The month of August was named for him. The Roman date was the ninth day before the Calends of September (our word calendar is derived from theirs).

Outside the town gates, stalls lined the roads, selling all sorts of things. The stall-holders cried their wares aloud like hawkers at a fair — sweets, pastries, melons in slices, grapes, coral charms, glass trinkets, sulphur matches, sandals and shoes, straw hats, tiny images of gods and goddesses. Also there were jugglers and acrobats, fortune-tellers, street musicians, gamblers rolling dice or playing the shell-and-pea game.

In celebration of the festival, Greek and Roman plays were advertised. Morning rehearsals were in progress at the Theatre. In the sports arena, several athletic events were getting under way. They would continue throughout the morning.

The streets of the town were jammed. The Forum was the busiest spot of all. Summer holiday-makers had come from Roma (the Latin and present Italian name for Rome) and Neapolis (the ancient Greek name for Naples — it meant "new city"). Peasants had come in from the country to see the sights. Poor women hurried with their task of carrying water in terra-cotta jugs from the public fountains. The jugs were carried on their heads, balanced on a coiled cloth. Rich women did not carry jugs because their houses had running water. They themselves were carried in litters borne by slaves. Or, if they walked, they were protected from the sun's heat by parasols held by maids.

All the snack bars had opened, selling bread of various kinds, cheese, wine, walnuts and almonds, dates, figs, and hot foods. Other shops displayed vegetables and grains, cloth, fishing gear, terra-cotta and bronze pots and jugs, glassware, bronze charms, and the handiwork of craftsmen and artists.

Workmen were busy, too. In the small workshops all sorts of things were being made. Cabinet-makers were putting together expensive inlaid wooden chests and furniture — hammering, sawing, turning their lathes. Artists called "mosaicists" were creating pictures with pieces of glass and glazed stone smaller than a fingernail. The dyers of cloth were busy at their vats. The cloth press, a machine with a worm screw almost as large

12

Right: Cord soles of beach sandals, only slightly scorched.

Below: Samples of the latest finds of fragile terra-cotta vases. The vase with a "face" may have been used in a child's room.

as a man, was in full operation. Goldsmiths and silversmiths were at work on jewellery and dishes. Marble workers were cutting, carving, and polishing marbles of many different colours. An artist was painting a group of cupids on a piece of wood to be set into a plaster wall. A sewing-woman completed a job of mending and neatly tucked her thimble and needle in her basket.

Inside the elegant houses overlooking the sea-front ladies who had risen late were being dressed by their maids. They had plentiful supplies of combs, hairpins, hair ornaments, mirrors, cosmetics, and perfumes. The ladies' jewel boxes contained necklaces, bracelets, anklets, earrings, brooches, and rings of gold and silver and precious stones.

In late morning the heat mounted. At the baker's shop of a man named Sextus Patulcus Felix, the baker and his helpers prepared to take from the oven the bronze pans containing cakes and tarts. That the cakes would rise was assured both by the baker's skill and a magic emblem over the door of the oven. Not far away, at another bakery where only

Silver back of a mirror. The fainting lady is thought to be Dido, queen of Carthage. She was left behind by the Trojan Aeneas, who suddenly sailed away. The love-god, Eros stands beside her knee, seemingly puzzled.

A Herculaneum mother supervises a maid dressing two young girls. They wear thin fabric in pastel shades. Their ornaments are bracelets, necklaces, earrings, and rings. Note that the mother's sandals are shaped to her feet. Note also the delicate glass pitcher under the graceful wooden table.

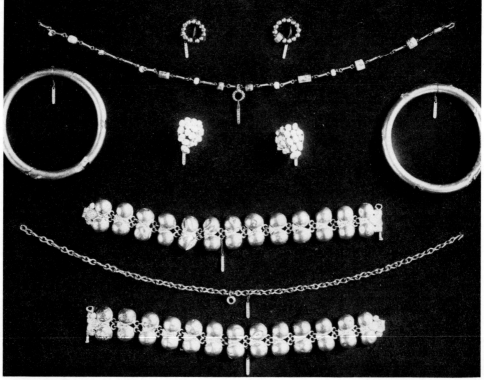

bread and dog biscuits were baked, flour was being ground by two donkeys no bigger than large dogs. Wearing blindfolds, the donkeys walked in an endless circle turning the heavy stone mill. They continually flicked their tails and ears against bothersome flies.

At a tinker's shop the tinker was heating his forge with bellows. A bronze candlestick and a statuette of the wine god Bacchus had been brought to him for repair. He set them temporarily on his counter. Near the Forum, at the shrine of the deified Emperor Augustus, the priests were holding a meeting. Within the shrine, in a small barred and locked room, a man flung himself on a bed in despair.

At the shop of the gem-cutter, a sick adolescent boy lay upon a finely-made wooden bed. As the boy was unable to get out of bed, chicken was brought to him to tempt his appetite. Close to the bed, a woman worked at a small loom, weaving cloth. As she worked she probably urged the boy to eat so that he might get well quickly.

The men's section of the Public Baths had opened. Attendants were assisting the earliest comers to undress. Clothing was folded and placed on the stone shelves. To make the water hotter, other attendants were stoking the boiler and raking out the ashes with a long iron poker. At the more luxurious Suburban Baths, on the marina, the steam room and hot and cold plunges were already in operation. Young men in one of the rooms were drawing some not-very-flattering pictures of their friends on a white plaster wall. They also wrote some bawdy verses.

In fact, all over town boys were drawing pictures and writing their names on walls. Some of them were Marcus and Rufus and Sabinus and Manius and Florus and Julius. One was called David. Older girls were writing about love, or how much they missed their boy friends. One was named Virginia.

Towards noon the athletic events in the arena were nearing completion. Boy victors in the stone toss, and perhaps swimming, were preparing to receive their olive wreath crowns. Like all the other athletes, they were naked and deeply suntanned, for Greek and Roman athletes did not wear

Left above: Close-up of a glass necklace and wooden jewel box found at Herculaneum. The ring has two serpent heads. They are simple and probably were not expensive. Perhaps they belonged to a young girl.

Below: Elaborate and expensive gold jewellery. Beautiful designs were made in silver, ivory, crystal, and ceramics, as well as gold. The goldsmith was one of the most highly skilled of ancient artists.

clothing. The victors' crowns were spread out on the broad marble table in the great hall.

The playing field of the sports arena was surrounded by a columned walk. In its centre was an olympic-size swimming pool in the shape of a cross. At the pool's centre, a giant bronze serpent sprayed water from five crowned heads. Officials, guests, and special fans sat in a shaded balcony on the north side, protected from the sun's glare. They rose and cheered the victors.

In almost every house lunch was being prepared. After lunch would come the long afternoon nap during the hottest part of the day. Wooden tables were set in shaded courtyards or gardens with fountains splashing. Romans preferred a light lunch. At an imposing house over the marina, waiters were about to serve hard-boiled eggs, bread, salad, small cakes, and fruit. Whole loaves of fresh bread, baked in round pans, had been placed on tables throughout Herculaneum. At one house, lunch was a little early — the bread had been broken and set down on the tablecloth. The first bite was surely in the diner's mouth.

Near the Forum a shipment of expensive glassware had just arrived. The glass was of beautiful design. It was packed in a special case carefully stuffed with straw. So eager were the owners to see their newest treasure that lunch was postponed while a servant began to open the case. The first protective layer of straw was torn away.

Left: Shortly before Vesuvius's eruption, someone placed a statuette of Bacchus and a lampstand on the counter at the tinker's shop. Both were bronze; both needed repair. The tinker got as far as setting out two ingots of metal (left) and heating up the forge with a bellows. The repairs remain unmade.

DAVID exactly as scratched on a wall by a Herculaneum boy nearly 2000 years ago. Girls' names also were written on walls. One was VIRGINIA.

Suddenly a violent, cracking sound split the air. The earth heaved and shook. The ear-shattering roars of a gigantic bull seemed to come directly out of the earth. The yellow sunlight turned abruptly to a brassy haze. The odour of sulphur and stinging gases choked nostrils. From the mountaintop a vast cloud in the shape of a mushroom billowed up into the sky.

Crazed with fright, dogs barked, asses brayed, horses whinnied, cats ran into hiding. People screamed that Vesuvius had blown apart. All who could rushed wildly into the streets.

One of the greatest and most terrifying natural disasters of all time had begun.

3 The volcano explodes

Warnings had not been lacking, but people had paid little attention. For some days mild earthquakes had been felt in the whole region of the Bay of Naples. The town of Pompeii, ten miles away on another flank of Vesuvius, had felt the shocks. The great city of Neapolis, farthest from the mountain, had felt them too. But in this area they were not at all unusual. People shrugged their shoulders and so were caught completely by surprise.

It is astonishing that so few mentions of the disaster have survived from antiquity. The only eyewitness description is that of Pliny the Younger (Gaius Plinius Secundus), who was seventeen at the time. Later he wrote two letters to the Roman historian Tacitus.

Tacitus wanted to know the story of the death of young Pliny's uncle, the famous naturalist known as Pliny the Elder. The Emperor Titus had recently appointed Pliny the Elder commander of the Roman fleet based at the little town of Misenum, a port on the Bay of Naples. It was even farther from Vesuvius than Neapolis. The Pliny family had a large country house, or villa, at Misenum. As an admiral, Pliny the Elder had ships and men at hand for rescue operations.

Young Pliny was very fond of his uncle, who had become his guardian after his own father's death. Though he wrote with restraint, he also wrote with great emotion. His letters are masterpieces. In the first he wrote:

> My dear Tacitus — You ask me for an account of my uncle's death, so that you may hand on a more reliable report of it to future generations. Thanks for this. I am sure that your report will make certain that he is never forgotten.

He was at Misenum in command of the fleet. On the ninth day before the Calends of September, at about the seventh hour (shortly after noon), my mother informed him that a cloud of extraordinary size and appearance had been seen. He had finished sun-bathing, his cold plunge, and lunch, and was at work on his books. He then demanded his sandals and climbed to a high point for the best possible view of the remarkable event.

The cloud was rising. Watchers from our distance could not tell from which mountain, though later it was known to be Vesuvius. In appearance and shape it was like a tree — the umbrella pine would give the best idea of it. Like an immense tree trunk it was projected into the air and opened out with branches. I believe that it was carried up by a violent gust, then left as the gust faltered. Or, overcome by its own weight, it scattered widely — sometimes white, sometimes dark and mottled, depending on whether it bore ash or cinders.

It was natural that a man of my uncle's scientific knowledge would decide that so grand a spectacle deserved close study. He ordered that a light galley be made ready. He gave me the opportunity of going with him if I wished. I answered that I would rather study, as he himself had assigned me some homework to do. Just as he was leaving, he received a note from Rectina, Caesius Bassus' wife . . . begging him to save them from their peril. Now he saw his expedition in a new light. What he had begun in the spirit of a scientist, he carried on as a hero.

He boarded ship with the intention of rescuing not only Rectina but others as well — for the charm of the coast had attracted many people. So he hastened in the direction from which others were fleeing, setting the helm for a course straight into the danger. Yet he kept so calm and cool that he noted all the changing shapes of the cloud, dictating his observations to his secretary.

And now ashes were falling on the ship, thicker and hotter the closer they approached. Also pumice stones and cinders — blackened, scorched, and scattered by the fires. Shallows suddenly were encountered, and landing was made difficult because the shore was blocked by rubble from the mountain. The pilot urged that they turn back. My uncle hesitated. Then he said: "Fortune favours the brave — steer towards Pomponianus!"

This man Pomponianus lived at Stabiae, on the far side of the bay (for the sea thrusts in between curving shores). There the danger was not yet immediate, though very near and very evident as it increased. Pomponianus had collected all his movables on board ship, with the intent to sail the moment the opposing wind died down. My uncle, favoured by this same wind, reached land. He embraced his anxious friend and cheered and encouraged him.

To calm fear by an appearance of unconcern, he asked for a bath. Then after bathing he sat down to eat with gusto, or at least (no less admirable) making a pretence of gusto.

From Mount Vesuvius, meanwhile, great sheets of flame were flashing out in more and more places. Their glare and brightness contrasted with the darkness of the night. My uncle, to relieve his companions' fears, declared that these were merely fires in farmhouses deserted by their peasants.

Then he lay down and slept. His sleep was unmistakable. His breathing was heavy and noisy because of his bulk and was heard by those who listened at the door. But the courtyard on which his room opened was being choked by a rising layer of cinders and ash. If he had delayed any longer it would have been impossible to escape. So he was wakened and went to join Pomponianus and the others, who had not slept.

They discussed whether to remain in the house or to go outside. The walls of the house were swaying with repeated violent shocks. They seemed to move in one direction and then another, as if shifted from their foundations. Nevertheless everyone dreaded the rain of pumice stones, though small and light, in the open air. After discussion they chose the second of the two dangers. My uncle was moved by the stronger reasons, and his companions by the stronger fears. With strips of linen they tied pillows to their heads and went out.

Elsewhere day had come, but there it was night — a night blacker and thicker than any ordinary night, though relieved by torches and flares of many kinds. They decided to go down to the shore, to see at first hand whether it was possible to sail. But the waves continued very rough and contrary.

There my uncle lay down on a sailcloth which had been cast ashore. He called repeatedly for water, which he drank. Then the approaching flames and the smell of sulphur put the others to flight. Aroused, my uncle struggled to his feet, leaning between two slaves. Immediately he fell down again. I assume that his breathing was affected by the dense vapours and that his wind-pipe was blocked. (It was narrow and weak, and often inflamed.)

When daylight returned, on the second day after my uncle had last seen it, his body was found. It was intact, without injury, and clad as in life. He seemed asleep, not dead.

Meanwhile mother and I were at Misenum. But that is not to the purpose, as you did not want to hear anything more than the facts of his death. So I will conclude . . .

But Tacitus did want to hear more. Pliny wrote a second letter, about what happened at Misenum:

. . . After my uncle's departure, I gave the rest of the day to study, the object which had kept me at home. Afterwards I bathed, ate dinner, and went to bed. It was a short and broken sleep.

For several days we had experienced earth shocks. They hardly alarmed us, as they are frequent here. That night they became so violent it seemed the world was not only being shaken, but turned upside down. My mother rushed to my bedroom just as I was rising. I had intended to wake her if she was asleep. We sat down in the courtyard of the house, which was separated by a short distance from the sea. Whether from courage or inexperience, I called for a book and began to read. I even continued writing in my notebook, as if nothing were the matter. . . . Though it was the first hour of the day, the light appeared to us still faint and uncertain.

Though we were in an open place, it was narrow. The buildings around us were so unsettled that the collapse of walls seemed a certainty. We decided to leave town to escape this menace.

The panic-stricken crowds followed us, responding to that instinct of fear which causes people to follow where others lead. In a long close tide they pushed and jostled us. When we were clear of the houses, we stopped, for we met fresh terrors. Though our carts were on level ground, they were tossed about in every direction. Even weighted with stones they could not be kept steady.

The sea appeared to have shrunk, as if withdrawn by the shaking earth. In any event, the shore had widened. Many sea creatures were beached on the sand. In the other direction loomed a horrible black cloud ripped by sudden bursts of fire. It writhed snakelike and revealed sudden flashes more intense than lightning. . . . Soon after, the cloud began to drop down upon the earth and cover the sea. Already it had surrounded and hidden Capri and blotted out Cape Misenum.

My mother now began to beg, urge, and command me to escape as best I could. A young man could do it. She, burdened with age and heaviness, would die easy if only she had not caused my death. I replied that I would not be saved without her. Taking her by the hand, I hurried her along. She came with reluctance, and not without self-reproach for getting in my way.

Ashes began to fall, but at first sparsely. I turned around. A frightening thick smoke, spreading over the earth like a flood, followed us. "Let's go into the fields while we can still see the way," I told my mother. I was afraid we might be crushed by the mob on the road in the darkness.

We had scarcely agreed, when we were enveloped in night. Not a moonless night or one dimmed by cloud, but the darkness of a sealed room without lights. Only the shrill cries of women, the wailing of children, the shouting of men were to be heard. Some were calling to their parents, others to their children, others to their wives, knowing one another only by voice. Some wept for themselves, others for their relations. There were those who, in their very fear of death, prayed for it. Many lifted up their hands to the gods. But a great number believed there were no gods — that this night was to be the world's last, eternal one.

A curious brightness revealed itself to us not as daylight but as approaching fire. It stopped some distance from us. Once more, darkness and ashes, thick and heavy. From time to time we had to get up and shake them off for fear of being actually buried and crushed under their weight.

I can boast that in so great a danger I did not utter a single word or a single complaint that could be considered a weakness. I believed that one and all of us would die — that made my own death seem easier. But the darkness lightened, and then, like smoke or cloud, dissolved away. Finally a genuine daylight came. The sun shone, but faintly as in an eclipse. And then, before our terror-striken gaze, everything appeared changed. Everything was covered by a thick layer of ashes, like an abundant snowfall.

We returned to Misenum, where we refreshed ourselves as best we could. We passed an anxious night between hope and fear — though chiefly fear. The earthquakes continued. Even so, my mother and I, despite the danger we had experienced and the danger which still threatened, had no thought of leaving until we should receive some word of my uncle. . . .

Eventually the sad news arrived. But young Pliny was fortunate in being so far away from the centre of the eruption. The pumice stones that dropped on Pompeii were nearly red-hot, burning or pitting everything they touched. The whole top of Vesuvius had been blown off. Most of this earthen matter, plus ash, settled on the area around Pompeii. In this way the city of twenty thousand people was covered to an average depth of seven metres. But no lava flowed over Pompeii. Though totally covered, it was not completely destroyed.

The fate of Herculaneum seems even more horrifying. It had been built on a little peninsula between two streams that flowed down the slopes of Vesuvius. Apparently, escaping steam condensed into water, and a river of volcanic mud oozed down the mountain. This mud was mixed with ash and pumice and had the thickness of treacle. It followed the two stream beds. Herculaneum found itself an island in a steaming sea of mud. Rapidly the mud rose and covered the town to depths ranging from twenty to twenty-eight metres. Not even a trace of its outlines remained.

The mud lava was hot, but not so hot as the pumice that fell on Pompeii. In some places the mud was hot enough to cook foodstuffs and turn wood into carbon. In other places it was only hot enough to scorch cloth. And in still others, wood, rope, eggs, and even fishing-nets were left almost totally unburned. In some houses wax tablets remained unmelted.

The force of the stream of mud also varied greatly. At some points its pressure felled walls and columns, smashed furniture, and carried away statuary. At other points, the mud rose so gently that it did not even smash eggs or move pots off kitchen stoves.

As the mud cooled, everything in Herculaneum was sealed tight. Occasionally it became as hard as limestone, but mostly it is similar to the light volcanic stone called "tufa." Tufa, sawn into blocks, is a building material in the Neapolitan area today.

The dead in Herculaneum raise puzzling questions. In comparison

Aerial view of Vesuvius exploding in 1943. Lava flow is in the foreground – true lava, not the hot mud that covered Herculaneum. True lava covered part of Herculaneum about three hundred years ago; the mud lava two thousand years ago.

with Pompeii they seem very few, for the dead in Pompeii have been estimated as at least a tenth of the population. From the position of bodies at Pompeii it appears that the volcanic gases were more deadly than at Herculaneum. Many seem unable to breathe, clasping hands over nose and mouth. Because they were covered with ash, it has been possible to make plaster casts, and last moments are almost as vivid as actually in life.

In Herculaneum the hot mud, which preserved almost everything else, destroyed the flesh of the dead. Only skeletons are left. They remain no less saddening than those of Pompeii. Two were found eight metres above the street level of the ancient town. They had boiled up in the mud.

The ash and hot pumice began to fall on Pompeii immediately after the explosion of Vesuvius. As the hot mud took longer to reach Herculaneum, its inhabitants had a better chance to escape. The earth shocks in Herculaneum were strong enough to topple statuary, yet buildings were not overturned. People were not trapped as at Pompeii. Those who waited to flee were lost once the mud had reached the level of the bridges over the streams.

At Herculaneum, as at Pompeii, there was not time to save precious objects. Herculaneum was left with its smallest valuables untouched: jewels, gold coins, fibulae (safety pins) of gold and silver, rings, silver plate, rare perfumes, legal documents. People ran away as they were — actors in costume, gladiators without helmets, bathers without clothes. The refugees who jammed the road to Neapolis resembled closely the refugees described by Pliny. But for the people of Herculaneum there was an extra horror: the onrushing mud.

The dreadful news of the eruption was flashed to Rome by the signal towers, the Roman way of sending telegrams. At once the Senate declared the whole region a "disaster area." The popular Emperor Titus helped provide relief from his own funds. He came from Rome to speak with survivors. A few people tried to dig at the lost towns, without results. No aid could make up for so total a loss. The towns seemed buried forever by Vesuvius.

In death, Herculaneum left behind the daily record of its life two thousand years ago. The record is more complete than any other site from antiquity ever explored by archaeologists. The mud sealed everything as if in plastic — a true time-capsule for us today.

4 Tales of Hercules and Herculaneum

Even two thousand years ago the people of Herculaneum thought of their town as an ancient town — just how old, nobody knew. Now, from bits of pottery (called "shards") it appears that Greeks settled in the area as early as the eighth century B.C. In the fifth century B.C., Greeks built a wall around Neapolis. They used enormous blocks of stone without mortar. Fragments of these walls may still be seen in the modern city of Naples.

Also in this area were the Italic people called Oscans. They built the earliest walls and towers of Pompeii, and the military signs above the gates remained in the Oscan language. Oscan names are scribbled in some of the houses of Herculaneum. So neither the Greeks nor Romans were "natives" of the Bay of Naples.

Were Oscans the original founders of Herculaneum? The Greek geographer Strabo, writing in the first century B.C., said yes. He added, ". . . next came the Etruscans and the Pelasgians, and thereafter the Samnites." Like the Oscans, all were Italic peoples — "natives." Their origins are unclear.

The Samnite houses in both Pompeii and Herculaneum tend to prove Strabo at least partially right. They were built in the old Italic style at least two hundred years before Christ. All the Neapolitan region, except the city itself, was under Samnite rule when conquered by the Romans. That was in the fourth century B.C. The Romans found the Samnites tough fighters, hard to subdue. The Samnites spoke Oscan, a language related to Latin. They were thoroughly familiar with Roman arms and tactics, but in the end they lost to superior Roman organisation.

Like so many ancient cities, the founding of Herculaneum is hazy. Legend has it that the town was founded by the Greek hero-god Herakles, or Hercules as the Romans called him. Evidently he was the protecting god (like a patron saint) of the town from earliest times. Venus, the goddess of love, was sacred to Pompeii.

In myth, Hercules was the best-loved son of Zeus (or Jupiter, to the Romans). Zeus was the most powerful of the gods on Mount Olympus in Greece, the king of heaven. Hercules was worshipped as half hero, half god. Hercules' mother was Alcmene, a mortal, the wife of a Greek general called Amphitryon. Zeus once tricked Amphitryon by assuming his form. So Alcmene, an ordinary human, bore the son of Zeus, a god. From birth Hercules had superhuman strength. Even in his cradle he was able to strangle two huge snakes. They had been sent by the goddess Hera to destroy him. She was Zeus' wife and was jealous of Hercules' mother. Hercules' Greek name, *Hera-kles*, means "famous through Hera." She never ceased to hate him and gave him the twelve mighty labours to fulfil.

It was after successfully completing the tenth labour that he came to Italy. In Spain he stole the huge red oxen of the three-headed giant Geryon and killed the giant. Then he displayed the oxen as he journeyed homeward. He visited many different parts of the Mediterranean, and one of his ports of call seems to have been Herculaneum. Many boys in the area are still given his name. In Italian it is called *Ercole*.

But the town of Hercules did not become important as a choice seaside residence until occupied by the Romans. In 89 B.C., Herculaneum joined Pompeii and other cities in a revolt against the Romans. The revolt failed. Both towns were quickly taken by the legions. The marks made by the Roman siege engines may still be seen on the walls of Pompeii. Some day when the walls of Herculaneum are uncovered, the signs of the Roman battering may be found there too. Afterwards, neither Pompeii nor Herculaneum had any need for walls, because of the long Roman peace. With peace came prosperity, and with prosperity came the construction of elaborate and beautiful town houses and the big country houses known as "villas."

The "Greekness" of Herculaneum was no barrier to its success with the Romans. All things Greek had become fashionable. The Roman upper classes spoke Greek as a second language. Roman buildings, art, and theatre often copied the Greek. And the craftsmen of Herculaneum were

Greek statue of Herakles, or Hercules, copy of an original carved in the fourth century B.C. As usual, Hercules carries a club and a lion skin. Statue stands in the Getty Museum, a copy of a Herculaneum villa.

Hercules's son Telephus had many adventures as a young man. This marble bas-relief, a masterpiece, shows Telephus as he sought and found the Greek hero Achilles. The sculpture probably belonged to Herculaneum's leading citizen, the Proconsul Marcus Nonius Balbus.

skilled in the Greek tradition. With its mild climate, beautiful position, and Greek origin, Herculaneum seemed perfect in Roman eyes.

As for Vesuvius, it was just another green mountain where magical nymphs and fauns were said to live. It was silvery with old olive trees. Its soil grew peaches and grapes of enormous size. No one could have believed that in reality it was a sleeping volcano. A few people with sharp eyes had noted its volcanic shape. The geographer Strabo climbed its peak in his old age and remarked that it was a "spent" volcano.

Nevertheless volcanic activity did exist in the Bay of Naples area. Only twenty miles from Herculaneum were the Phlegraean Fields, known since remote antiquity for their smoking caverns and geysers of steam and water. Here in a grotto at Cumae lived the Sibyl, a sorceress famed for difficult riddles. Here was the infernal Lake Avernus, with waters as black as those of Hades. Here was the legendary entrance to the Underworld, a cavern in fact dangerous with poisonous gases. Here too was the fashionable resort, Baiae, where hot mineral waters gushed from the earth and the

Romans built baths of the utmost luxury. Yet no one associated all this with Vesuvius, in spite of its shape.

Though forgotten as a volcano, Vesuvius had another kind of fame. Here the rebel slave Spartacus had battled with the Roman legions. Spartacus was the strong and intelligent gladiator who in 73 B.C. led a full-scale revolt against the Roman masters. The slaves had no historians to present their case, but it is known that before Spartacus two major uprisings of slaves had taken place. The story of Spartacus is full of excitement, bravery, and tragedy.

At one stage of the revolt, Spartacus sought safety with seventy followers in the rugged, wooded hollow on the summit of Vesuvius. The Romans thought the slaves were trapped. Instead, the rebels plaited chains of wild vine, and, unseen, let themselves down on the steep side. Stealthily they approached the Roman camp, surprised and captured it.

Before the revolt was over, the seventy had swelled to seventy thousand. But Spartacus lost. After brilliant victories the slave armies were finally crushed. Spartacus was crucified, and the Appian Way outside Rome was lined with the crosses of his followers.

So, from the past of sleepy little Herculaneum no one could have guessed its future. No one could have guessed that historically it was to become one of the most important cities of the world. All because of a sleeping volcano.

But first many, many years had to pass.

5 The lost town and how it was found

Human memory, even for disasters, is short. Not only the sites, but the names of the buried cities were forgotten. The writings concerning them were destroyed or lost. The Dark Ages had set in. The great buildings of Rome and Greece were destroyed or fell apart. The libraries were ransacked by the invading barbarians. Even the letters of young Pliny disappeared. For a thousand years people lived in filth, ignorance, and misery.

Vesuvius did not again have a major eruption. But the volcano did not permit its savage nature to be forgotten. In A.D. 203 it erupted for a week, and in 306 for several days. In 471 began a series of eruptions which lasted for three years, eruptions so severe that ashes were blown for hundreds of miles. The first recorded lava streams were in 513 and 533. From 1305 to 1308 lava burst at intervals from the sides of the mountain. In 1631 lava — true fire lava, not mud — reached the site where Herculaneum had been, burying it even deeper. In 1759 a terrifying eruption occurred. It is said that Vesuvius once vomited seaweed and boiled fish.

In modern times the eruptions, though irregular, have continued. They have followed much the same pattern. The most dramatic was the eruption of 1943; it took place the day the Allied forces landed nearby during World War II. Then the volcano grunted like a living beast and tossed showers of rocks bigger than a human head. Lava also flowed in the direction of Herculaneum, but stopped short.

Despite the eruptions, the lower slopes of Vesuvius remain planted with orchards and vineyards. A new Pompeii of a sort now exists, chiefly for tourists. Where beautiful Herculaneum once stood sprawls an ugly slum called Resina. For many years the people who lived there had no idea that an ancient city lay under their feet.

Herculaneum's long sleep was not disturbed until the year 1709. A lucky chance led to its discovery. In the town of Resina was a monastery. The monks needed a well. In sinking the well a workman struck an upper row of seats in Herculaneum's Theatre. He brought up rare and beautiful marbles.

It happened that nearby an Austrian prince was building a big and luxurious villa. As he had need for marble, the find was called to his attention. From the quality of the marbles the Prince realized that the well-digger had stumbled upon an important structure dating from antiquity. He cared nothing for the building itself, but only for the materials it might yield for his own project. He lacked even the slightest archaeological interest.

He ordered that the well be deepened and exploratory tunnels dug. All sorts of marvellous discoveries were made. The plunder continued as long as the Prince's villa was under construction, a period of seven years. Finally the Prince gave up his treasure hunt and left Herculaneum to its gravelike peace. The Prince never realized that he had made one of the most important archaeological strikes of all time. He did not know that an ancient theatre, completely intact, had been discovered.

Not until 1738 was the Theatre identified, and shortly thereafter the name of the town. An inscription was found that proved the site was Herculaneum. At last the town of Hercules would return to the map.

The King of Naples at that time was Charles III, a Spanish Bourbon. He appointed not a scholar but a Spanish military engineer to begin digging. He could hardly have made a worse choice for an archaeologist or a better one for a treasure-hunter. The engineer enlarged the original shaft of the well. He made a gaping hole, letting in daylight on a few of the Theatre's upper seats. He enlarged existing tunnels into galleries and began new tunnels in all directions.

Soon the diggers realized that they were in the hidden town itself. From this busy ant-hill came new finds of dramatic appearance and great value. Everything was carried to the Royal Palace. This was the beginning of the collection that eventually was to rest in the National Archaeological Museum in Naples, where it can be seen today.

The military engineer was guilty of many stupidities. For example, he removed bronze lettering from walls and statue bases without first reading the inscriptions. The result was a heap of meaningless letters like alphabet soup. Everything was haphazard. Digging was done on whim, now this way and now that way. Luckily daily reports were issued, and a diary was kept in Spanish. But no record of the details of each find — its place, position, relation to other objects — was kept. No street plans or building plans were made. The burrowing went on everywhere about the town: along streets; over roofs; through walls, wooden doors, vaults, paintings, mosaics, everything.

The undermining, smashing, and snatching continued until the appearance of a young Swiss architect named Karl Weber. He introduced some order into the chaos. For several years he had the opportunity to continue his more systematic tunnelling. He faced serious obstacles. One was the continual opposition of the military engineer, who lied about him to the King and went so far as to remove scaffolding so that galleries would collapse. The other obstacles came from the nature of the site.

The passages, deep underground, were little different from those in a mine. Water and slime dripped from the walls. The work was slow and dangerous. Earth and rubble were carried away in little straw baskets. Gases constantly threatened suffocation. The only light came from feeble oil lamps or smoky torches. Normal sculpture seemed to take on horrible shapes and were thought to be devils. No wonder that little knowledge was gained of the general character of the town. All in all, the work of the Neapolitan diggers was truly a thirteenth labour of Hercules.

In 1765 those tunnels which had not been refilled were closed and all digging stopped. Interest was shifted to Pompeii, where sensational new finds had occurred. Quick rewards of gold and silver and statues were the object. Nobody thought of digging up an ancient city for its own sake to find out just how our ancestors had lived.

Many years later another King of Naples became interested in Herculaneum. Young Francis I proved deeply moved by Pompeii. Moody and romantic, he loved to take moonlight strolls among the ruins. He began to brood about the town buried under the suffocating mass of mud. In 1828 he ordered a renewal of digging at Herculaneum.

King Francis felt that Herculaneum ought to be brought out into the open. Accordingly the tunnels were ignored. Work was begun in an area that did not lie under the crowded streets of Resina. Hacking away with great effort at the solidified mud with hand tools, progress was slow. A few houses were uncovered. At once people began to speak of "Ercolano" as if it were an ordinary Italian town.

After seven years of the new attempt, the results did not seem equal to

Dining room of the "House of the Stags." Two sculptured stags are being brought down by hunting dogs. Couches and tables were removed by the Bourbon tunnellers; they missed the stags.

the efforts. Digging methods were so crude that the ancient houses were wrecked as they were revealed. They appeared as almost total ruins. Rich finds were rare. So the King lost interest, and the project was dropped.

For a long span of years not a pick or a shovel was seen at Herculaneum. Finally in 1869, under the king of a united Italy, Victor Emanuel II, excavations were started again. But the physical conditions of work — pitting strong arms and backs against the resistant mud — had not improved. Again progress was slight. As the digging approached the jumbled houses of Resina, a new difficulty arose: the flinty opposition of the Resina landlords. They were not interested in the knowledge gained through archaeology. They preferred the bursting slums of the present to the livable but empty houses of the past. In 1875 they forced a stop. It seemed that Herculaneum was to remain forever buried.

Work did not begin again until 1927 — a full two hundred and eighteen years after the initial discovery. The Italian government decided to dig at a steady pace, as already had been done at Pompeii. New machines, new methods, and skilled men were at hand. Archaeology had grown from a hobby into a science.

At last the whole town of Herculaneum seemed to have a chance of returning to the light of day . . . intact.

6 The modern dig

The first diggers did more damage to buried Herculaneum than the volcanic mud. We may be thankful, today, that they had so little success. Now all the technical tools of modern archaeology can be brought to the task.

Note the following list of equipment needed for today's most limited dig. It amazes those of us who have had no training in archaeology. And how it would amaze the early tunnellers! Here it is:

Clinometer for measuring slopes. Plane table for measuring angles. Alidade for showing degrees of arc. Prismatic compass for taking accurate bearings. Levelling staves marked in centimetres for measuring elevations. Templates for recording the curves of mouldings. Brooms, brushes, and mason's tools for cleaning architectural finds. Zinc plates and sodium hydroxide pencils for electrolysis of coins. Measuring tapes of all sizes. Mechanical-drawing instruments. Trowels. Marking pegs. Cord. Squared paper. Filter paper for taking "squeezes" of inscriptions. Catalogue cards. India ink. Shellac. Cardboard boxes. Small cloth bags. Labels. Journal books, field notebooks, and technical manuals. Cameras. Picks, shovels, refuse baskets.

For a major dig like Herculaneum, even more is needed and amazement increases. Compressed-air drills. Electric saws. Bulldozers. Narrow-gauge railway. Dump trucks and related equipment.

Also needed, for restoring damaged buildings and objects, are: Skilled masons. Mosaicists. Fresco-painters. Marble workers. Bronze casters. Carpenters. Cabinet-makers. Useful, too, are: Chemists, for analysing content of jars and bottles, paints, kitchen pans. Metallurgists, for analysing corroded or mixed metals. Glass experts. Physicists, for dating with the radioactive isotope carbon 14. Historians, for their knowledge of background history. Language scholars — at Herculaneum, experts in Latin and Greek, Oscan, and occasionally Egyptian and Etruscan.

The modern excavations have the aim of restoring the town to its original appearance. A citizen of Herculaneum, returning after almost two thousand years, ought to be able to find his house much as he left it — familiar objects all in place, food in the cupboard, flowers blooming in the courtyard, fountains running. All this of course is very difficult to do.

Everybody asks the question: "How big was Herculaneum?" And the answer is that nobody really knows. The population estimate of four to five thousand is based on the number of seats in the Theatre. The actual area covered by the town can only be a guess, because the Bourbon tunnellers never succeeded in groping very far under the streets of Resina. Some archaeologists have estimated the town's area at about twenty-two hectares. But the answer must be left to future excavation.

Aerial view of the small excavated portion of Herculaneum. Tenements of today's town, Resina, can be seen above, upper left. Much of the ancient town lies under the streets of Resina. Right: The archaeologists' map of the excavations.

Not much is known about the town as a whole. Some parts have been made clear by the tunnels. Other parts have been much better defined by the open excavations. The town plan, with its orderly rectangular blocks, is similar to ancient Neapolis. It is therefore Greek. It contrasts sharply with Pompeii's irregular plan and the tangled streets of the oldest section. Herculaneum's streets were paved with Vesuvian stone (still used in Naples).

Unlike the streets of Pompeii, Herculaneum's streets rarely show ruts worn by wheels of heavily laden carts. Nor do they have stepping-stones to keep pedestrians' feet dry on rainy days. In fact, the stepping-stones were not needed, because Herculaneum boasted an excellent drainage system. It was a large underground sewer expertly constructed. Pompeii lacked such a sewer.

Herculaneum's ample water supply flowed from the mountains through aqueducts. Many private wells and cisterns continued in use. A water-tower proves that city water-pressure was adequate. A filtration system,

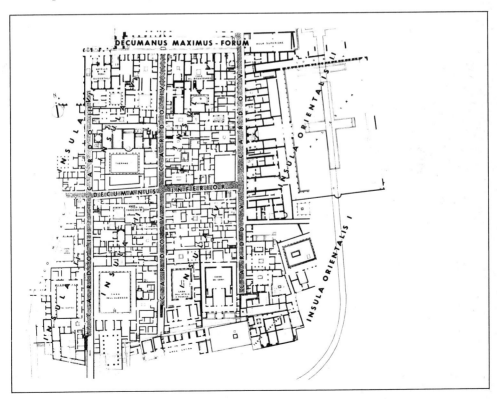

One of the Roman water valves that still functions. It is bronze. Some pipes were lead. Pure water was brought from the mountains to Herculaneum through stone aqueducts. Roman engineering was not surpassed until modern times.

to purify the water, was included. Most modern cities would be fortunate to have water equally pure. Though the public latrines have not yet been located, no doubt they were like other Roman latrines. That is, they were flushed with a constant flow of water. Also their rows of marble seats were handsomely decorated. Romans did not feel the need to conceal natural body functions.

The private houses of Herculaneum are more advanced in their design than most of those in Pompeii. Houses were important possessions in both towns. They were built not only to last for generations, but for centuries. They were designed for a single family, its dependants, and heirs. Often they were kept up-to-date by changes in layout or decoration — remodelling. Apparently everybody liked old houses, but not old-fashioned houses.

The old-fashioned Italic house had followed a regular form. It had a living room (the atrium), with a basin for catching rainwater in the centre (the impluvium). It was covered by an inward-sloping roof from all four sides, with an opening in the centre (the compluvium). Terra-cotta drains collected rain from the roof for the basin and also for a cistern. Originally the roof opening let the smoke escape from the fire on the hearth. The marriage bed was placed in an adjoining room (the tablinum) shielded by curtains. Sometimes a separate dining space (the triclinium) was built, and sometimes not.

Statuettes of the household gods, the Lares and Penates, were kept nearby on a shelf, or in a shrine or niche (the lararium). Sometimes they were painted on the wall. They represented the spirit of the house itself and the spirits of the ancestors. Devout old Romans made daily offerings to them — a portion of the food on the hearth. The Romans always remembered and honoured their dead.

In Herculaneum the old-style houses were often greatly changed. They were so "modernized" that we would find them comfortable houses to live in today, as we shall see. Also discovered in Herculaneum was a large apartment house of several storeys, and a typical cheaply constructed house to meet the needs of the Roman population explosion.

The rising mud performed several important functions for which archaeologists are very grateful. In Pompeii the upper portions of houses collapsed under the weight of ash. But in Herculaneum the mud supported the upper portions. It is possible to walk along a pavement shaded by the overhanging upper storeys of buildings, still having almost the exact appearance of two thousand years ago.

Also, the mud preserved wood. Sometimes its temperature was scorching, and wood was burned black (carbonized). But sometimes wood seems untouched. Everything from stairs and shutters to tables and beds has been preserved. Herculaneum proves that the amount of wood used in ancient buildings was much greater than formerly supposed. And it proves, too, that no finer furniture has ever been made anywhere in any time known to us.

The modern excavations revealed additional information about the people of Herculaneum. They seemed much engaged in fishing, if the amount of nets, hooks, floats, and other gear is any sign. The shops, snack bars, and taverns were in plentiful supply, as might be expected in a seaside resort town. Also many skilled craftsmen sold their wares. In the back streets of Naples their descendants are still to be seen: wrought-iron workers, wood-carvers, mosaicists, gilt applicators, gold- and silversmiths.

Attitudes towards love are revealed in the paintings and statuary that people chose for their houses and gardens. The scribbles on the walls (graffiti) tell us even more, because Romans and Greeks were uninhibited. Nudity was not considered improper or shocking. In paintings men are portrayed as deeply bronzed by the sun, women as creamy-white. Scenes and situations frowned on by puritans were not frowned on by Herculaneans. They liked lusty jokes.

Their point of view was one of easy-going naturalism. Every part of

Left: A Herculaneum street leading into the centre of the town from the marina (Cardo IV on the map). Original wooden beams remain in the roof overhangs. Modern Resina rises at the end of the street.

Above: Same Herculaneum street, looking towards the marina. Cypress trees now grow where the sea used to be. The house in the right foreground is the elegant "House of the Wooden Partition." Next door is the cheaply built "Trellis House." It was occupied by two plebeian, or working-class, families.

Fishing was important in Herculaneum, as is proved by surviving gear. Here is a fishing net in amazingly good condition after nearly twenty centuries. To the right are bronze tools for repairing nets. Today the shape is the same, but they are made of plastic.

human life, even the most earthy, was portrayed everywhere — on shop signs, walls, paintings, bell-pulls, jewellery, dishes. Statuary was, if anything, even more graphic. Almost all forms of love were accepted as normal. All human behaviour was reflected in the gods themselves. The gods had human emotions and human virtues and vices. Their stories were told in paintings on hundreds of walls, and often in statuary.

Not much is yet known about the organised religious life of Herculaneum. Not one temple has been discovered. In fact the "Shrine of the Augustales" is the only religious structure so far found. This was related to the cult of "deified emperors." A temple to Hercules the protector must surely exist. A graceful life-size marble statue of Venus was discovered, but nobody now knows exactly where. She wears a thin garment, expertly handled by the sculptor. An inscription states that the Emperor Vespasian restored the temple of the "Mother of the Gods" — the eastern goddess Cybele. But nothing more has been found. Statuettes of gods and goddesses have

46

Romans were very fond of Eros, the god of love. Here the boy-god is shown dozing against a tree trunk. This is a fine sculpture of marble. The broken parts were found in several different places.

The patroness of Herculaneum's sister-city Pompeii was the goddess of love, Venus — or Aphrodite as the Greeks called her. This life-size statue found at Herculaneum is very similar to one found at Pompeii. Both are copies of a Greek original carved in the fifth century B.C.

47

appeared in plenty: Jupiter, Bacchus, Mercury, and, in many forms, Venus.

A wall painting shows white-robed priests of Isis performing their rituals. Isis was an Egyptian cult with mysteries of death and resurrection. Puzzling was the recent discovery of a statue of the Egyptian sun god, Aton. The worship of Aton as the *one* god was proclaimed in Egypt in the fourteenth century B.C. by the Pharaoh Amenhotep IV, or Ikhnaton, brother and husband of the glamorous Nefertiti. The Pharaoh failed, and the priests soon went back to all the old gods.

Most curious of all is the imprint of a cross in a simple Herculaneum apartment. It appears to have been hurriedly ripped from the wall. Is it genuine evidence that the cult of the Christos had followers in Herculaneum? (Or, as the Romans said, "Chrestus.") We will look at this discovery in greater detail in the next chapter, for it may be unusually important.

The modern excavations have uncovered many wonderful things. But it is still in the dark eighteenth-century tunnels that you feel the full horror of the eruption — and how enormous is the unfinished task of freeing Herculaneum from the mud lava.

7 How well-to-do people lived

Today we surprise the people of Herculaneum, so to speak, because we walk into their houses uninvited. So we learn the most about their lives. Nobody can put up a false front, tidying rooms normally in disorder, or hiding the pictures and statuary. Everything is exactly as it was, including unerased doodles on the walls.

If we approached Herculaneum from the sea on that fateful August morning we would have seen a charming little town. We would have noticed first the sunlight glittering on gilded bronze statuary mounted on impressive public buildings. Then the deep green of cypress, palms, and oleanders in the shady gardens. Drawing closer, we would have seen a cluster of varied buildings along the marina, including statues and fountains.

Above, on top of the town wall, was a row of houses. This was the old pre-Roman wall, no longer needed, facing the marina. The houses on the wall were much more colourful than houses today. They were patrician homes, built overlooking the sea for the breeze and the view. They were equipped with terraces, arcades, balconies, hanging gardens, fountains, arbours, statues. Often their columns were painted red. Their roof tiles were a dark yellow terra-cotta. Their mosaics glinted with blue and gold. They were luxurious and elegant houses, perfectly designed for hot summer days and the seashore.

Now the sea is far away from its former boundaries, driven back by the waves of mud. Thanks to the new excavations, it is possible to approach Herculaneum from the bay side over land. The view is not too dissimilar to what it was nineteen centuries ago. Houses crown the wall as in the past. Gardens have been restored and fountains flow. A visitor almost expects a figure in Roman dress to appear, wave, and call a friendly greeting.

Houses of the wealthy built on the town wall overlooking the Herculaneum marina, as they appear today. They glow with many bright colours: red-tiled roofs, blue and gold mosaics, red and yellow columns.

A steep incline leads up through the Marine Gate (Porta Marina) into the town. Entrances to the patrician houses face on various streets. Portals open directly on to the pavements.

One of the best-preserved is the "House of the Mosaic Atrium" (Casa dell'Atrio a Mosaico). Inside the portal is a vestibule, or entrance hall, with a small room on either side. The right room is for the cook, the left for the doorkeeper (ianitor — the American word janitor) and his dog.

Here the mosaic floor is a geometrical design of large black and white rectangles. It was forced into wavy shapes by the enormous pressure of the mud. In the centre of the main room, the atrium, under an old-style opening in the centre of the roof, is a white marble rainwater basin. This basin, like the floor, has been forced out of shape by the weight of the mud. Opening at the far end is another large and handsome room. The statuary that undoubtedly adorned these rooms is missing. It might have been

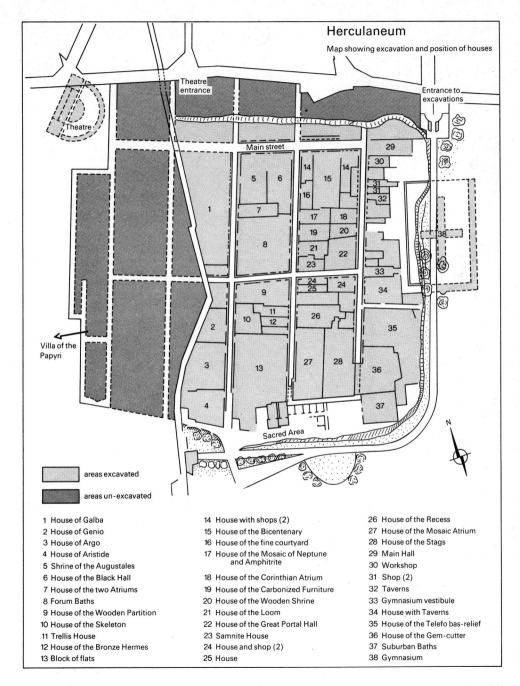

Herculaneum

Map showing excavation and position of houses

Theatre entrance

Entrance to excavations

Theatre

Main street

Villa of the Papyri

5   6
14   14
15
16
1
7
17   18
19   20
8
21   22
23
9   24
25   24
10   11   12
2   26
3   13   27   28
4
36
37
29
30
31
31
32
38
33
34
35
36
37

Sacred Area

N

areas excavated

areas un-excavated

1 House of Galba	14 House with shops (2)	26 House of the Recess
2 House of Genio	15 House of the Bicentenary	27 House of the Mosaic Atrium
3 House of Argo	16 House of the fine courtyard	28 House of the Stags
4 House of Aristide	17 House of the Mosaic of Neptune and Amphitrite	29 Main Hall
5 Shrine of the Augustales		30 Workshop
6 House of the Black Hall	18 House of the Corinthian Atrium	31 Shop (2)
7 House of the two Atriums	19 House of the Carbonized Furniture	32 Taverns
8 Forum Baths	20 House of the Wooden Shrine	33 Gymnasium vestibule
9 House of the Wooden Partition	21 House of the Loom	34 House with Taverns
10 House of the Skeleton	22 House of the Great Portal Hall	35 House of the Telefo bas-relief
11 Trellis House	23 Samnite House	36 House of the Gem-cutter
12 House of the Bronze Hermes	24 House and shop (2)	37 Suburban Baths
13 Block of flats	25 House	38 Gymnasium

The "House of the Mosaic Atrium" illustrates the terrific pressure of the volcanic mud. Both mosaic floor and marble basin were distorted into a wavy pattern. The house was stripped of furniture by the Bourbon tunnellers.

swept away by the flow of mud down the slope towards the sea, or more probably it was removed by the early tunnellers.

As the owners wished to take full advantage of the site, a second house, in effect, was built on the very edge of the wall. The two sections were then connected. The architects were thinking about the climate. Here were hot summer days with brilliant sunlight; winter days sometimes rainy and overcast, sometimes clear but cold with a strong northeast wind; cool spring and autumn days with bright sunlight; rarely ice and snow. Closed walks between the two sections of the house were the architects' answer.

A garden was laid out and walks constructed on either side. That

The original fountain still spurts in the garden of the "House of the Mosaic Atrium." Plants of the same types grow in the same spots as two thousand years ago. Walks were enclosed by large glass panes in wooden frames.

which faced the cold east winds was brick-enclosed, with small windows for light. The opposite walk was all glass, with large sheets of glass held in place by narrow strips of wood. The original wood, though carbonized, is still there. The glass was broken.

In the garden the native plants of two thousand years ago have been replaced. Many roots remained to guide the archaeologists. The paths, where peacocks once strutted, are gravelled as before. A jet of water splashes upward in a rectangular marble basin where goldfish swim. The original lead pipe to the fountain is still visible, still works.

Behind the glass walk is a pleasant small sitting-room overlooking the garden. The walls, with two landscape paintings, are coloured an azure blue. One painting shows "The Punishment of Dirce" — a mythical woman who was tied to a bull as punishment for her own cruelty. The other painting is "Diana Bathing" — showing the goddess of the hunt at her bath. On either side of the sitting-room are two bedrooms with red walls and stuccoed ceilings. In one is a round three-legged table with each leg carved as a cat's head. On the table is a round loaf of bread. Both table and bread are carbonized.

Not far from the edge of the town wall, with a sweeping view of the sea, an imposing dining-room was built. Its furniture has disappeared. But here once rested the usual three couches and low table for relaxed dining. Each couch held three persons. In early times, women sat at table while men reclined. Later, both reclined.

In such a house as this, the table would have been of bronze with a marble top. The couches would have been wood inlaid with silver or gold and mother-of-pearl, amber, or ivory. For extra comfort, the couches sloped upward at one end. Sometimes the frame was curved in the form of a swan's neck. The cushions were of various colours and made of the finest soft materials. Dishes, knives, and spoons were probably of silver. Forks were not used by the Romans at table. Meat was cut in advance by a servant called the "scissor."

The room's wall decorations have not survived. Perhaps they were soothing pastoral scenes or paintings of fish or game, as in other patrician dining-rooms. The Romans greatly enjoyed good food and liked everything about dining to be agreeable.

Outside the dining-room, facing south for the warmth, is a covered arcade — or, as said in Italy, loggia. Just beyond is a small uncovered terrace for sun-bathing. The Romans called it the solarium. At either end of the loggia is a small shaded room for afternoon rest. These little rooms were intended to catch both the sea breezes and the view. They were agreeable spots for a nap during the heat of the day.

Some of the objects found in this house are now displayed in various rooms: a kitchen colander with holes pierced in a beautiful design; bronze bowls and glassware; a hatchet; decorations for a horse bridle; a wax tablet; ladles for soup; bells; oil lamps; door handles of bronze; a statuette of Venus; a fishhook; bronze candlesticks; perfume flasks; a bowlful of dates; a lead water-tank intricately decorated.

Probably in this house, as in many Herculaneum houses, money and

Top: Canvas folding stool with decorated bronze legs. Greeks and Romans did not like to clutter their houses with unnecessary furniture. Folding stools were often used. The wood and fabric of this stool have been restored.

Below: Sundial from a Herculaneum garden. Roman days were divided into twelve equal hours from dawn to sunset. Thus summer hours were longer than winter hours. Water clocks functioned both day and night.

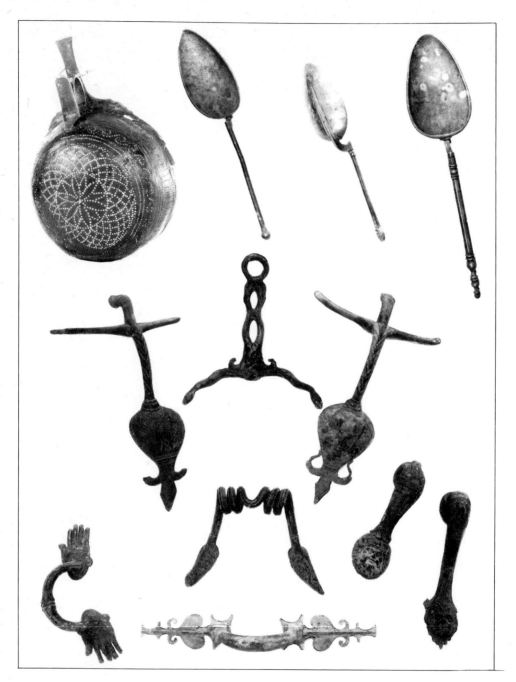

Top left: Bronze kitchen colander. Note the eleborate geometrical design. Romans liked even the least important household objects to be beautiful.

Top left: Silver spoons. Forks, as we know them, did not come into use until the Middle Ages. Romans rarely used knives at table, as meat was cut in the kitchen by a servant called the "scissor."

Left: Door handles and pulls for chests of drawers. All are made of bronze.

Above: Drinking glass and glass jar. Glasses were often coloured. Jars were used for marinated vegetables, jams, and jellies. Huge numbers have been excavated.

jewels were found. In the house next door, cooking utensils still remain in place on the kitchen stove. In another was a wooden cradle, like a modern doll's cradle, still holding the bones of a baby. (How could it have been left behind?) And in the latrine is a famous graffito on the wall, signed by a doctor who said he was the physician of the Emperor Titus. Many fine pieces of sculpture were discovered, including the "Drunken Hercules" which pokes fun at the hero-god.

Wooden cradle containing the bones of an infant, just as it was found in a patrician's house. Why the baby was left behind is one of Herculaneum's unsolved mysteries. Perhaps the parents were not at home, and the slave nurse fled.

Top left: Glass spoons, similar to Chinese soup spoons. These were found covered by straw in a box only half-unpacked. They are a very recent find, very rare.

Below left: Charcoal stove in the kitchen of the "House of the Stags." Cooking pots remain just as they were left almost two thousand years ago. Lunch was ready to be served. It still could be, as the stove functions.

Only a few people, however, could afford the costly sites and costly houses along the wall above the sea. The rest of the patricians lived in less imposing houses on ordinary streets. And as hard times came, the owners tended to become small landlords. They split up their houses into flats and shops for the rents. So we see that not all Roman patricians were rich.

Part of the "poor" patricians' history can be read in the "Samnite House" (Casa Sannitica). It was built during Herculaneum's pre-Roman period, at least three centuries before the eruption. When the house was new it had space — a courtyard, a loggia, a garden, many rooms. But in Roman times the house was changed. The open-air loggia was bricked in. A new door was made on the street, giving access by steep stairs to a tiny flat to let. Next the courtyard and garden were sold, leaving the owners

60

Left: One of the oldest houses in Herculaneum was the "Samnite House"— at least three hundred years old when Vesuvius exploded. It was built by a Samnite family, as a name scratched in the Samnite language indicates. After the Roman conquest, the upstairs columned loggia was bricked in to make a separate flat for a tenant.

Above: The "House of the Wooden Partition". The wooden panels slid back and forth to separate the two rooms at will. Handles are made of finely worked bronze. The marble table in the foreground stands just as it did at the time of the eruption.

only what remained of the ground floor. The house had fallen on hard times.

Today a small painting remains. It is "The Rape of Europa" — when Zeus transformed himself into a powerful white bull and carried away the princess Europa. On another wall is a name scratched in Oscan letters, reading from right to left: SPUNES LOPI. Was this the idle work of the son of the original owner — perhaps one day when he was in bed with a cold? Or did the house remain in the hands of a Samnite family until the day it was submerged in mud?

Now in the house is a broken statuette of Venus putting on her sandals; fragments of wooden table legs carved in the form of dog's feet; a bowl of

Left: A pair of dice, identical with ours today.

Right: Not sweets, but black and white tokens for playing a game, perhaps like backgammon. Ten black and ten white tokens range in size from large to small. Backgammon is known to be at least two thousand years old.

biscuits. Another wall-writing is not in Oscan but in Latin: "Let love burn here!"

The front of the "poor" patrician "House of the Wooden Partition" (Casa del Tramezzo di Legno) is the most completely preserved of any house in Herculaneum or Pompeii. With its little windows on the street side it might easily be a present-day house in certain parts of Rome. The main difference would be that the wooden roof beams of the Herculaneum house are carbonized.

This was a big house. It ran the entire length of the block with entrances on separate streets. It was a typical noble house of pre-Roman days. The rooms are high-ceilinged and decorated to the top. But the most striking

62

Mosaic game "board." It has 110 alternating black and white squares, in contrast with the 64 of present chess and draughtboards.

feature, which gives the house its name, is the large wooden partition used to close off the two largest rooms.

The partition was originally composed of three handsomely panelled double doors. The central section was destroyed by the careless tunnellers, who bored straight through mud, wood, and all. The doors' reconstruction in their original place is a triumph. The two thousand-year-old wood swings on two thousand-year-old hinges. The bronze handles are just as before. The bronze supports, designed like ship's ornaments, still hold lamps. The ancient carpenters and woodworkers, though lacking power tools, clearly would need no lessons from us today.

The rest of the house is in keeping. In the garden, the owner painted on the walls flowers, shrubs, and ducks — all as lifelike as the real models. On the wall of one room is scribbled an angry complaint at somebody

63

nicknamed "Mouse." He (or she), said the writer, was "a low-life."

During the later excavations many small objects were found in this house. We see the handles for a chest of drawers exactly like ours today. Also the same are: strap hinges, pincers, bowls, ladles, glass jars, belt buckles, bells, a lock and key, beads, a hatchet-hammer, blue chalk, chickpeas. The perfume flasks are somewhat different. The needle is bronze, not steel. The straw from a broom is straw, not plastic. The black and white "backgammon" chips are a little different from ours, but the dice are exactly the same. The sandals for horses' hooves (to prevent slipping on stone) are woven of cord, like some beach sandals today.

But the most astonishing object of all is an ordinary piece of bread. It was broken from a loaf by a person who was just beginning lunch when Vesuvius exploded. Now it is fused to a portion of the tablecloth, and carbonized.

In 1938 one of the most important of the patrician houses was uncovered. It is called the "House of the Bicentenary" (Casa del Bicentenario) because it was found exactly two hundred years after the beginning of organised exploration of Herculaneum. This house has caused much argument among archaeologists and historians. In one of its rooms was found what may be the mark of a Christian crucifix.

The room was on the upper floor. It was set apart from a small rented flat. In the centre of one wall was a white plaster panel. In the centre of the panel was the shape of a cross. Either a shelf or a crucifix had been ripped away, apparently in haste. If a shelf, it was of unusual shape. A wooden cabinet, like a small oratory, was found below the white panel. The cabinet had a platform in front, as if for praying on the knees. Also in the room was a terra-cotta jug in one corner, a plate, a bowl, a pot with a handle, and a lamp. That was all.

Most scholars now believe that the mark was made by a crucifix. Not all agree. The Apostle Paul landed nearby in A.D. 61, and a Christian cell at Herculaneum might have been the result of his teaching. Nothing similar has been found from any site dating from the first century A.D. So the Herculaneum find is truly historically significant if it shows that as early as A.D. 79 the cross had become a Christian symbol. Someday new evidence may be found.

Right: The "Christian chapel" as it appeared when unearthed. The wooden cabinet (oratory) was not yet cleared of hardened mud. The cross had been ripped from the white plaster.

Above: Colonnade peristyle of the "House of the Bicentenary" — the house where the slave girl Justa lived. Visible above is the door to the room now called the "Christian chapel." Records of Justa's law suit were found in rooms to the right. A lemon tree grows in the courtyard.

Right: The high quality of Roman cabinet-making is shown by this wooden shrine for household goods. The lower portion was a cupboard for odds and ends. The small restored portion is clearly indicated.

Besides the patricians, one other group was well-to-do in Herculaneum: the merchants and commercial people. Today we would call them the middle class. All the middle-class houses show the same problem: lack of space. Big houses cost too much for middle-class purses. In decoration, however, these people had the same taste as patricians. That is, they decorated their houses in the same way, with wall paintings, mosaics, statues. Often they were successful; but sometimes they could not afford quality artists or craftsmen, and their decorations were crudely done.

68

It is from the middle-class houses in Herculaneum that most of our knowledge of Roman wooden furniture has come. Roman houses, like Greek houses, were sparsely furnished, but each piece of furniture tends to be of very high quality. Thanks to the solidified mud, we can actually touch the same furniture used by the ancient inhabitants of Herculaneum. Most of the wood is carbonized, and the finish and upholstery have disappeared. All the same it is easy to imagine the appearance of the original, because the whole structure is there before our eyes.

In the middle-class "House of the Wooden Shrine" (Casa del Sacello in Legno) was preserved an extremely rare specimen of ancient furniture — a combination cupboard and shrine. The shrine, with its double function, indicates Roman thriftiness. Its form is that of a temple, though it reminds us of a large doll's house. The double doors open to reveal the statuettes of the gods within. Below, closed shelves held, and still hold, perfume flasks, buttons, pincers, a strigil (for scraping off oil and sweat at the baths), dice, a glass fruit bowl, a dish of garlic, and a statuette of Mercury.

In another room is a good example of a small round table. It now holds a woven straw basket and a cup of pine nuts. Upstairs, a large number of unreadable wax tablets were found under a bed. The owner of the house was Lucius Autronius Euthymius, whose personal seal survived.

The house next door has a list of gladiators who fought in the Arena (the amphitheatre). This is interesting to find in a town Greek in origin. The Greeks generally did not favour the custom. Gladiators fought other gladiators or wild beasts to the death before large crowds. The Romans acquired this type of spectacle from the Etruscans.

But to return to furniture. Bedroom furniture was especially well-preserved in all houses, rich or poor. There were a few double beds, but most were single. In upper-class houses, beds were more elaborate. Often their legs were shaped by lathes and ornamented with bronze or silver. Most beds had wooden panels at the head and on one side, to protect the sleeper from the damp of the stone wall. Mattresses probably were of fine-combed wool, or, in summer, a sweet-smelling grass. Usually they

Top left: Divan discovered in the "House of the Carbonized Furniture." Originally it was upholstered and had many soft cushions. The small table was beside it, set for lunch. The dishes can be seen on the floor of the glass case. Note how the wall fresco decorations were cracked by earth tremors.

Below left: Restored wooden bed, showing spindle legs and sculptured bronze ornaments. Mattresses rested on slats, sometimes on slung ropes. The vessels are chamber pots, for use at night.

The sea-god, Neptune, and his wife, Salacia (Latin *sal*, salt), are the subjects of this brilliant many-coloured mosaic. It decorated one entire wall of an outdoor dining-room. The owner had a cereal shop.

were placed on slats, not parallel but in square or rectangular forms, but some beds supported the mattress by ropes slung between the frames.

In the "House of the Carbonized Furniture" (Casa del Mobilio Carbonizzato) is an unusually fine dining couch, or divan. It is in its original place, with a round wooden dining-table standing close by. The divan has a high back and sides of richly veneered wood. It was upholstered and cushioned. After eating, the occupant had only to stretch out for a nap. The table is still set with dishes for lunch.

The "House of the Mosaic of Neptune and Amphitrite" (Casa del Mosaico di Nettuno e di Anfitrite) is one of the most interesting of all Herculaneum's middle-class houses. It also has a connecting shop, remodelled from part of it. The name was given to this house because of a mosaic showing the god of the sea, Neptune, with his wife. Amphitrite was her Greek name. Her Roman name was Salacia, the goddess of salt water. In the mosaic, Neptune is naked and his wife is partially draped. They are done in glittering gold, against a huge conch shell. It is a work of art fit for a palace.

The House of Neptune is unusual because it is *not* intact. Its wall on the street was either shaken down or pushed out by the mud. It is sheered off as if Vesuvius had planned to place the contents of the house on display, like department store windows. On an upper floor, visible from the street, is a bedroom with its wooden bed, bronze candelabrum, and marble table — all perfectly preserved. To the right, the latrine is laid open. The pipe from the seat to the sewer is visible all the way. We will examine the shop later.

Within the house, all the walls are painted with skilful frescoes. On one wall is scribbled a list of wine deliveries with their dates. On another is a list of spelling words to be learned by a schoolboy. In the entrance hall is a bust of Hercules and a statuette of Jupiter. In the open summer dining-room, the owner made up for lack of a garden by many-coloured mosaics of floral designs. No living flowers could equal their brilliance.

We can only imagine with what regret the owner fled from his house. And how upset he must have been when his front wall collapsed! Perhaps he remembered that Neptune was not only god of the sea, but earth-shaker too. No matter how well a man lived, he was helpless before the gigantic uncontrolled forces of nature.

8 A country treasure house

Very, very rich Romans lived in the luxurious country house now called the "Villa of the Papyri" (Villa Suburbana dei Papiri). Large suburban houses with gardens were known as "villas." This one gets its name from the books in its library, written on the Egyptian paper called "papyrus." The villa remains buried, just outside Herculaneum.

Luckily, a detailed plan was drawn by the Swiss architect Karl Weber during the eighteenth-century tunnelling. The plan gives us a clear idea of the size of the villa and its gardens. Today we can see in the Naples Museum many of the treasures which were brought up. Even more will be learned when the villa is rescued from the twenty to twenty-six metres of hard mud still entombing it. Weber's tunnelling was far from complete. Modern Italian archaeologists hope to finish the job.

The villa was a low structure of red-tiled roofs and columned walks surrounding gardens, fountains, and pools. It stretched at least one thousand Roman feet (about 250 metres) along an embankment above the Bay of Naples. Below was a beach equipped with private docks and boathouses. Stairs led upward by terraces to the villa level. The entrance had impressive columns.

The old-fashioned atrium had become a large entrance hall. In the middle of its black-and-white mosaic pavement was the familiar rainwater basin, but here the marble pool was surrounded by eleven statues. The statues were satyrs — creatures half goat and half man — pouring water from wineskins. Some were cupids pouring water from the mouths of dolphins. Jets of water all around the pool transformed it into a fanciful fountain. In a wall niche was the large basin of another fountain. The heads of thirteen bronze tigers spurted water from their mouths. In other niches

72

were busts of royal Greeks and statuettes of fauns. One was a dancing faun and another was a bearded satyr playing a pipe.

The entrance hall opened directly into a square courtyard with ten columns on each side. In the middle, streams of water spurted from conch shells into a long, narrow pool. Here was found the bronze head of "The Lance Bearer," a famous athlete.

It is the finest existing copy of the head of the original by Polyclitus — the fifth-century B.C. Greek sculptor who first worked out the ideal proportions of the human body. It is signed by a copyist who lived in the first-century B.C. — Apollonius of Athens. Fresh garlands of flowers were daily hung on the bust as tribute to the athlete. The original statue was a full-length nude. Because of its perfect proportions it was one of the most renowned sculptures of antiquity.

Elsewhere was found the head of an Amazon, the legendary woman warriors. Oddest find was a bronze portable sundial. Most practical was a bronze charcoal brazier for winter days. The legs are three aroused goat-footed laughing satyrs, each with his left hand outstretched in warning not to touch. It has become famous today, but probably was not considered unusual in its own time.

The exit to the grand courtyard led through a columned room similar to the Acropolis in Athens. Here stood an archaic marble statue of the goddess

A replica of the luxurious Villa of the Papyri has been built in California, U.S.A. It is the J. Paul Getty Museum.

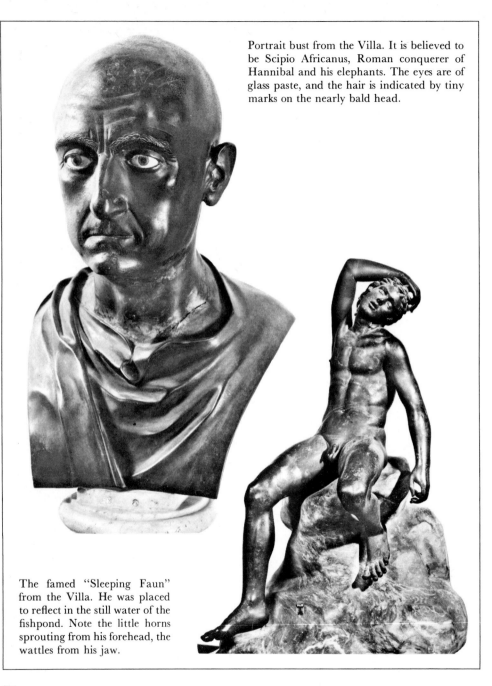

Portrait bust from the Villa. It is believed to be Scipio Africanus, Roman conquerer of Hannibal and his elephants. The eyes are of glass paste, and the hair is indicated by tiny marks on the nearly bald head.

The famed "Sleeping Faun" from the Villa. He was placed to reflect in the still water of the fishpond. Note the little horns sprouting from his forehead, the wattles from his jaw.

Athene — a statue from very ancient times. Her appearance was rather stiff and awkward. Bronze portrait busts were set in two rows. One portrait may be the Roman hero Scipio Africanus, conqueror of Hannibal and his elephants. He is shown as almost bald. The line of his hair is marked by a kind of tattoo on the skull. Scattered on the floor of this room were scrolls of papyrus and wax tablets, apparently dropped by some agitated human hand.

Outside was the great garden courtyard, a rectangle 100 metres long and 37 metres wide. Sixty-four columns surrounded the courtyard. On one side was an enclosed, windowed walk for wintertime. In the centre of the garden was a fish pond as large as the swimming pools in the Imperial Baths in Rome: 66 metres long and 7 metres wide.

Here were found enough sculptures to supply a whole art gallery. Concealed underground was an aqueduct and the complicated hydraulic system used to supply the house, the ponds, and the fountains with water. At the end of a gravelled pathway stood a "rotunda" — a columned, round garden-house of marble. It had a round marble floor with triangle designs. You can now see the floor in the Naples Museum, for it was brought up piece by piece.

The sculptures, for their quality and fame, are worth attention in detail. When not originals, they were expert copies of masterpieces.

In the garden, among flowers, were two bronze deer, a jumping piglet, and various busts. One bust was the blind poet Homer. At the curve of the pool the extraordinary "Sleeping Faun" was found. The naked young faun is a life-size bronze placed to reflect in the water. He sits with his right arm thrown back over his head, drowsing. From his forehead, under thickly curling hair, sprout short horns. From the sides of his cheeks dangle little goat wattles. The Faun is considered one of the greatest sculptures of antiquity. But who was the sculptor? No one knows. There is no signature.

Under the columns were five life-size statues of young women. They wear a simple Greek garment draped from the shoulders. The group is now called the "Dancers of Herculaneum." They are not dancing, but just what they are doing with their rhythmic arm movements nobody can decide. Their eyes are made of glass paste. The hems of their bronze garments show traces of colour. Their meaning of two thousand years ago is now totally lost.

In the garden were still more sculptures. One marble was an earthy animal group, "Pan with a She-Goat." It was intended to laugh at the

Bronze deer, one of several sculptured animals taken from the garden of the "Villa of the Papyri." Others were a twin deer, a leaping piglet, a goat with the god Pan.

animal nature of man, though some people find it shocking. The most important sculptures in the garden were: two boy wrestlers, the "Drunken Silenus" (Silenus was the foster-father of Dionysus and the leader of the satyrs), and the world-famous "Hermes in Repose" (the Roman Mercury). All are of bronze, all life-size.

The wrestlers are young naked boys about to close with one another. Their bodies are modelled with lifelike grace. Their eyes of glass paste seem real, and their lips show traces of red colouring. The "Drunken Faun," on the other hand, portrays a once-athletic body in middle age. The Silenus — or old faun, as he is sometimes called — lies drunk next to an inflated wineskin. Raising himself on his left arm, he snaps the fingers of his right hand. He is laughing hilariously and telling everyone that he is not old yet. So realistic is this rascal that a couple of teeth are missing. Again the sculptor is unknown.

An unquestioned masterpiece is the "Hermes in Repose." The young

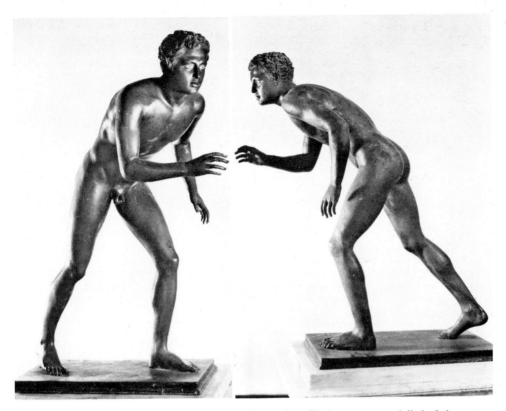

The "Boy Wrestlers" are about to close in friendly combat. Their eyes are modelled of glass paste, and even now red paint may be seen on their lips. They are Greek sculptures, dating from the fourth century B.C.

Hermes is naked except for wings strapped to his ankles. Relaxed and graceful, he is pausing a moment on a rock before again taking flight as the messenger of the gods. His lips, too, are touched with red. This statue may be the actual handiwork of the Greek sculptor Lysippos, favourite of Alexander the Great.

What of the total haul? From this one villa came ninety pieces of sculpture including the greatest single collection of ancient bronze statuary ever found. Copies of many were made for display in Athens, home of great Greek sculpture. The originals were stolen by the German Nazis during World War II, but have been recovered.

Even if no sculpture had been found, the library would have marked the dig as one of the most amazing feats in the history of archaeology. This

"Resting Hermes," or Mercury — life-size bronze recovered from the Papyri Villa as part of a treasure trove of great sculpture. Note the delicate wings bound to Mercury's ankles to give his swiftness as the messenger of the gods.

was the first ancient library ever to be discovered. No one dreamed then that the sands of Egypt or the Dead Sea caves might also conceal ancient manuscripts.

It was not until the third year after the discovery of the villa that a tunnel reached a small room with an elegant marble floor. It was clearly a study. Close by was another small room. It had wooden shelves, stacked with what appeared to be cylinder-shaped charcoal briquettes, enough for many, many barbecues. The briquettes proved to be rolls of papyrus. The rolls, 1787 of them in all, had been badly scorched by the hot mud.

Despite the fact that the manuscripts were unreadable, the find excited the world. The problem was how to unroll and read. In the eighteenth century no scientific methods existed for such a task. So King Charles III of Naples called in a painter, whose efforts resulted in many scrolls damaged and only a few words made clear. The attempt was given up.

Later a specialist in old manuscripts made a new effort. A machine was constructed to unroll the papyrus. It unrolled a scroll at the rate of less than one centimetre per hour. After four years of trial and error, the machine produced results. Three scrolls were unwound. Scholars read part of the *Essay on Music* by a Greek philosopher named Philodemus.

Slowly new scrolls were examined. So excited was the world that the King of England, George II, hired scholars to come to Italy and lend a hand. And such personages as Pope Pius IX and the Czar of Russia visited Naples to see the books for themselves. Today eight hundred scrolls still remain unread in the National Library of Naples.

The general character of the villa's library soon became clear. The scrolls were an almost complete collection of the works of one man — the philosopher Philodemus. Most were in the Greek language. A few were in Latin. The hoped-for unknown writings of the great classical masters were missing — a severe disappointment for everyone. How could the owner of so stupendous a villa have collected so narrow a library? It seemed that only a patron or publisher would stock the works of a single author.

This provided a clue as to the possible ownership of the villa. It was known that a wealthy Roman called Piso was the patron and supporter of Philodemus. Piso's daughter, Calpurnia, was Julius Caesar's wife. So the Herculaneum villa probably belonged to Piso, and Julius Caesar probably often made visits there. These deductions are made almost certain by one of Philodemus' poems. He calls himself Piso's "pet friend." Some day a new inscription may prove the point.

When the villa's statuary was brought above ground in the eighteenth century, superstitious peasants gathered about the tunnel entrances. As the naked pagan "demons" appeared from the earth, the peasants crossed themselves in fear. No doubt many more "demons" await.

Much of the villa is untouched. Yet to be discovered are the decorations, furniture, statuary, jewels, and private articles of the living quarters. Yet to be discovered are the children's playrooms. Also the kitchen, workshops, servants' quarters, garden sheds, boathouses, and all the gear necessary to the operation of a huge country house.

It can safely be said that amazing discoveries remain to be made in the Villa of the Papyri. Some day we may read about them in newspapers or hear about them over radio or television, as the dig goes on.

9 How working people lived

Roman wealth was not produced by magic, but by ordinary working people and by slaves. The houses, shops, and workshops of merchants and craftsmen in Herculaneum are easy to recognise. These people were called "plebs" — short for plebians, as opposed to patricians.

The small merchants often lived in small houses that were connected with or close to their shops. The craftsmen often lived in cramped quarters to the rear of their workshops. Sometimes, too, the ground space was used for both working and selling. As for the slaves, they were given the smallest rooms, or those near the kitchen.

Two very unusual plebian buildings have been uncovered in Herculaneum. One was a block of flats for many low-income families. The other was a cheaply constructed two-family dwelling. They are unusual because no others exactly like them have been found anywhere, though they must have existed by the thousands. These two structures are important in the history of city construction, or "urban design," as we now say. The two-family dwelling is the only known complete example of a cheap, rapid-construction Roman housing unit. The details of construction were written down by the architect Vitruvius as early as 16 B.C.

The block of flats is big and impressive. It was over eighty metres wide, and its remaining height is about four storeys. The upper storeys were destroyed in the eruption. Five- and six-storey blocks were common in Rome. Some were taller, though the Emperor Augustus had limited their height. They were built entirely of brick (or stone) and wood — no steel. Most city people lived in blocks of flats. Except for their decorations, they must have seemed very much like blocks of flats in any modern city.

The ground floor of the Herculaneum building was divided into shops.

The upper floors were reached by at least two different stairs. Details of the water system are not clear. The large vaulted sewer has been explored. Its size is so great that it would have served many flats. It is easy to imagine washday with clothing hanging from the balconies. And as today in Naples, baskets would have been let down on cords from upper windows for small packages. Neapolitan children still love to play games and tricks with these baskets.

The two-family house, in contrast to the massive block of flats, is as fragile as a bird cage. Strangely, it survived in far better shape than the larger building. It stands next door to the patrician House of the Wooden Partition and could hardly be in greater contrast. Were the children of these two houses allowed to play together? Normally, adult Romans of all classes rubbed shoulders, so perhaps the children did too.

This little structure is called simply the "Trellis House." It is nothing more than a wooden skeleton of square frames. Each square is filled in by stones and mortar crudely thrown together. Inside partitions are flimsy laths of cane, thinly plastered. An economical, fast method of construction was needed to meet the Roman population explosion, and "trellis work" was the answer. The architect Vitruvius pointed out its disadvantages: lack of permanence, dampness, danger of fire. It would astonish him to know that one such house has survived two thousand years.

Some of the steps in the wooden staircase are still usable. Upstairs bedrooms have retained their red wall paint. The wooden bedsteads, the wooden clothes cabinet, the wooden cupboard with utensils and statuettes of the household gods — all remain in their places. So do the marble tables. Only mattresses, linen, and clothing are missing. But the original rope, slightly scorched, is still wound on the original windlass for the well.

The working people or small traders who lived here reclined at meals like patricians or the rich middle class. This is proved by a still-intact dining couch. Also intact is a doll carved of wood and part of a marble "oscillum" with a horse carved on it. The round oscillum was about the size of a dinner plate. It was hung from the ceiling in such a way that it could be spun, or "oscillate." It must once have hung in a patrician house. When broken, it was probably flung on the junk heap, only to be retrieved by a boy who lived in the Trellis House and brought home as a trophy. Even broken, it would have been fun to spin.

One of the games played by children and adults was similar to our backgammon. The set found here is identical with the set found in the

Children's games were very similar then and now. Here cupids are playing hide-and-seek. This little painting was one of a series decorating a hallway. Another painting shows blindman's buff.

Head carved from wood, possibly for a large doll, or possibly the work of an amateur wood carver. Discovered upstairs in the modest "Trellis House."

Windlass and rope for a well, coiled exactly as it was left on the morning of the eruption.

patrician house next door. The glassware is good. The drawing pins are still sharp enough for a school desk. On one wall someone wrote that his friend Basileus still remains in the town of Puteoli. If the former tenants could return, they would find it easy to take up living in their house again.

Scattered among the patrician homes in Herculaneum are many small houses attached to shops. The shops and workshops vary greatly in size and equipment. All the small merchants were not equally successful; all the craftsmen not equally in demand. It appears that competition was fierce among them. Similar shops can still be seen on the back streets of many Italian cities today.

The largest shop yet discovered in Herculaneum was just across the street from the entrance to the sports arena (the Palaestra). It was a corner shop — a good spot, like a snack bar near a modern football ground. The counter was faced with irregular pieces of different coloured marble. Eight large jugs (dolia) are embedded in the counter itself. They contained

Girls playing knucklebones, a game similar to dice. The girls' names were: Latona, Niobe, Phoebe, Aglae, Ilearia. The drawing is on white marble and is signed by the artist, Alexander the Athenian.

various cereals and vegetables, as has been shown by chemical analysis. Another larger jug perhaps held olive oil. Other jugs and amphorae (jugs with pointed bottoms) may have been for other oils or sauce. A stove behind the counter was in use. Varied dishes were kept simmering in terra-cotta casseroles over the charcoal fire. The food was probably eaten while standing in the shop or taken away by the customer.

Interior view of the most complete ancient shop ever discovered. Merchandise was cereal, olive oil, and oddly, hot soup. The wooden railing and partition are the original. The lamp hangs where it always hung. The huge jar (dolium) is full of grain for sale.

A spare room was rented by a wine merchant, for a large number of wine amphorae were found there. The merchant may have been one of those wine exporters whose amphorae were marked in the Oscan language. Such amphorae have been found by skin divers in sunken Roman ships.

The snack bars and wine shops had a standard arrangement, always similar to the shop described above. Many counter displays remain intact: walnuts, almonds, dates, figs. In addition, cheeses, raisins wrapped in lemon leaves, and delicious little cakes were sold. Hot drinks also were served. The Romans were very fond of mulled or spiced wines of many sorts, often sweetened with honey.

One of Herculaneum's snack bars has become especially well known because of its advertising. The phallic-god Priapus was boldly painted

Above: Close-up of a Herculaneum scale still containing merchandise. The buyer never completed his purchase. Note the mortar and pestle to the left, with a small drain hole for liquids.

Top right: Walnuts, kernels intact, from the counter of a snack bar. Romans liked to nibble walnuts with a little wine.

Bottom right: Samples of many fragile items surviving at Herculaneum: Top row, left to right: bread (baked in the same shaped loaf as in Italy today), rope, pine nuts. Bottom row, left to right: cloth (part of a roll), seeds, webbing.

behind the counter for all passers-by to see. The symbol of Priapus was believed to be effective against the evil eye, so any customer would be sure to be in luck. On the counter are still displayed the original walnuts set out for sale. In the rear wall is a spy hole, through which the proprietor could keep an eye on the shop. Possibly he had trouble with small boys who snatched walnuts and ran away.

A few doors down the street is the shop of a cloth merchant. In this shop the modern excavators made an exceptional find: remnants of the

ancient cloth itself. Now it is displayed in a glass case, and the wavelike design is clearly visible.

Roman garments, with the exception of short tunics, used yards and yards of material. Quality had to be high so that clothing would be long-lasting. Cloth was of wool, linen, or cotton — silk was an expensive luxury. In remote Republican times, the main colour was white or near-white. Coloured robes or tunics were worn only by foreigners or slaves. But with prosperity Roman women got tired of the sameness of their clothes, and finer materials and more and more colours were introduced. Later, men began to wear colour in their dinner clothes.

To meet the new demand it was necessary for the dye industry to expand. Even in so small a town as Herculaneum several dye works have already been found. They are easy to recognise by the type of furnace used to heat the dye. Clothes cleaners, "fullers," also have been found. Among other substances, they used the alkaline clay now called "fullers' earth."

Like the dye works, the bakeries are marked by their ovens. Even today Italian towns are still served by small neighbourhood bakeries. Bakers work during the pre-dawn hours. Loaves of bread are still made in exactly the same shapes as in Herculaneum. Most are round with division marks so that the loaf can easily be broken into sections. It is much better than factory-made bread.

The largest bakery found in Herculaneum used a charcoal oven identical with today's Neapolitan pizza oven: a large stone igloo. Its iron door is tightly closed, and the lead water-tank used for dampening the oven broom still stands nearby. The long wooden pallets used for removing the loaves have disappeared. Perhaps this oven was used in daytime for baking dog biscuits, a Roman speciality for their pets.

Here the grain was milled in the courtyard. Two mills were turned by tiny blindfolded asses, walking continuously in a circle. Their bones were found where they died in harness. Behind the bakery were both stables and the baker's lodgings. The latter were handsome vaulted rooms with fine pavements and wall decorations.

The name of one baker in Herculaneum is known: Sextus Patulcus Felix. His seal was found in his shop. He specialised in cakes. We know because twenty-five bronze baking pans of various sizes were left hanging from a rack or in the oven. When he ran away, he also left a great deal of money.

This is the bakery of Sextus Patulcus Felix. His baking pans hang on the back wall. The grain mills (right) were turned by tiny donkeys wearing blindfolds. Bread was baked fresh every morning before dawn, as it is now in Italian towns.

In the front part of the shop were the flour mills. To one side, in a sooty two-storey vaulted room, was the round oven and its lofty chimney. It is perfectly preserved — you could cook in it today. Though this baker's name was "Lucky" (Felix), he took no chances with his luck. Over the oven door he placed two phallic good-luck charms, side by side, to make sure his cakes would rise. And in the dough room (the mixing bowls are still on the shelf) he placed two more charms. But as he fled no doubt he cursed his luck.

Not far away was a luxury shop: a gem-cutter, or as we would call him,

The skeleton of an adolescent boy remains on this couch. Perhaps he was paralysed with polio. Nearby are chicken bones from his lunch. A woman was working on the small loom. The couch and the loom stool were handsomely decorated with inlaid wood. This was the prosperous "Shop of the Gem-Cutter." The boy and many precious gems were left to the rising mud.

a jeweller. About this shop we know a great deal. The owner had a considerable supply of gems, which he displayed on a wide marble table. In the rear of the shop, he left behind a portrait bust with a damaged nose. He also left behind a child. In a small room an adolescent boy lay on an expensively decorated bed. Nearby, a woman sat on a square inlaid wooden stool, weaving on a small loom. Probably she was a slave or an old freedwoman. For the sick boy's lunch, chicken had been prepared. Portions had been brought to his bedside. At the moment Vesuvius exploded, everyone ran except the boy.

How did it happen that in the moment of panic the boy was abandoned? Were his father and mother absent? Was the woman too old and too feeble

One of the most important finds of ancient technology was this cloth press. It was made of wood with a central worm screw almost as large as a man. Its resemblance to the earliest printing presses is striking. Now it is enclosed in glass.

to carry him away? Was he partially paralysed, perhaps with polio, so that he himself could not leave the bed? While the mud rose he must have waited frantically for the rescue that never came. His bones still lie in the bed, the chicken bones in the plate — equally preserved.

From another shop came one of the rarest and most important technological finds of antiquity: a cloth press. The machine is two metres high and seventy centimetres wide. It is constructed of hard wood, including its large worm screw. The most exciting fact about the cloth press is its appearance: it is very similar to the printing press invented thirteen hundred years later. It could have been used for printing either wooden blocks or movable metal type. Actually the basic principles of printing were already understood, but not as type. The bronze name seals are similar to type. The letters are raised from the surface and read in reverse. (They were used as rubber stamps are today.) But somehow the press and type remained apart. This now seems a tragedy, because the printing of multitudes of cheap books might have profoundly changed the Roman world and helped prevent its decline and fall.

All these shops suffered damage from the eruption or from the Bourbon tunnellers. Fortunately for us, one shop came through almost untouched. It is the best-preserved and most completely equipped of all those discovered in Herculaneum or Pompeii. It was part of the House of Neptune and Amphitrite. As it has a back door opening into that house, we may assume that the owner of the glittering mosaic courtyard was also the owner of this thriving shop.

The merchandise was cereal and wine, with some of the cereal sold precooked. Wooden scaffolds holding wine amphorae and wooden staging for shelves remain intact. The cross-hatched wooden grill separating a part of the shop remains unbroken. A coiled rope hangs on a pin and a lamp hangs from its usual hook. Charcoal in the stove is prepared for a rekindled fire. The plumber has repaired the drain in the sink. The usual containers are full of cereals. Beans and peas are on the counter for sale.

The shop seems open and ready for business. At the ping of a coin, surely the proprietor will appear. Or maybe, like his fellow citizens, he is having an extra-long summer afternoon nap?

10 Justa - story of a Roman slave girl

Eighteen wax tablets, unmelted, were found in a room near the Christian "chapel" in the House of the Bicentenary. The tablets were sealed in such a way as to be tamper-proof. They were not only unmelted, but readable — and therefore an exceptionally exciting find. They proved to be records of a lawsuit. Involved were a pretty slave girl and a man named Gaius Petronius Stephanus.

The story began about the time of the great earthquake of A.D. 62, when a baby girl was born in the quarters of Gaius Petronius Stephanus. He was one of the tenants in the house. The child was called Justa. The mother's name was Vitalis. The father's name, if known, was not acknowledged. Slaves were not permitted to marry.

The mother, Vitalis, had been bought as a slave by Gaius Petronius, probably as a gift to his new wife at the time of his wedding. He had married a freedwoman known as Calatoria Temidis. Gaius Petronius was a member of the lower middle class, and it was not unusual that he should marry a freedwoman

Nor was it unusual that the slave woman Vitalis eventually should be freed. Perhaps she purchased herself, paying also a freedom tax equal to five per cent of her valuation. Once free, Vitalis assumed her master's name. Thereafter she was called Petronia Vitalis. And the child Justa was accepted into the master's household, and — in his words — "brought up like a daughter." For ten years or more all went well.

But the peace dissolved at the birth of children to Gaius Petronius. Friction arose between his wife Calatoria and the freedwoman Petronia Vitalis. They argued and bickered. Petronia Vitalis, as a freedwoman, could no longer be forced to remain in the house. She chose to leave. She wanted a home of her own and was willing to work hard for what she wanted.

Gaius Petronius and his wife refused to allow the girl Justa to go with her mother. They looked upon her as their own, they said. She was now grown-up, intelligent, and pretty, and they wanted to keep her.

Indignant, Petronia Vitalis brought suit for her daughter. After a time, the case was settled with the award of Justa to her mother. However, Gaius Petronius had to be repaid for the cost of Justa's food and upkeep. Luckily, Petronia Vitalis had saved a considerable amount of money. Immediately she made the payment and took Justa home. Mother and daughter were very happy.

Their happiness was short. Petronia Vitalis died, leaving Justa all alone. At about the same time, Gaius Petronius died too. This seemed to be the end of the story. Not so.

The widow of Gaius Petronius, Calatoria, brought suit to recover Justa and all the property she had inherited from her mother. Calatoria claimed that Justa was a slave, because she had been born while her mother was still a slave. And as slaves could not own property, all Justa's property therefore belonged to Calatoria.

Justa had spirit. She fought back. No written evidence existed for either side. The act of freeing a slave had once been a complex process. It was always legally recorded. But when the large majority of the population became slaves, the rules were changed. A letter, or even a few words by the master in the presence of witnesses, did the trick. In freeing Vitalis, Gaius Petronius had remarked merely that the woman was no longer bound. No record was kept of the date. Nor, if Vitalis bought herself, did she have a receipt. So the sole proof rested on witnesses who supposedly were present at the time. And witnesses were easy to buy.

The suit was brought before the local Herculaneum magistrates. They declared that they lacked authority over the matter, so the case was sent to Rome. There witnesses were called and every statement recorded. A parade of pros and cons followed, cancelling one another. One of the witnesses against Justa was an illiterate man who claimed to know the inside story from Gaius Petronius. But his talk was so garbled that even with aid it was impossible to put his account into credible, much less grammatical, form. His evidence, nevertheless, was admitted. Then the case bogged down, a swamp of confusions.

Suddenly a new witness appeared — a witness who cleared the air. He spoke in favour of Justa. He was Telesforus, the administrator-manager-foreman who had served Gaius Petronius for many years as a freedman. Though he still served Calatoria, he dared testify against her. His statement was matter-of-fact and precise. He had handled the discussions for the return of Justa to her mother, he said. It was then admitted that Justa had been born after her mother was freed. The court in Rome, he said, should now accept this fact.

For all of Justa's and Telesforus' pleas, the court was not willing to make a rapid decision. The judge wished to think it over. And over. And over again.

The hearings in Rome began in the year we call A.D. 75 and were carried over into A.D. 76. When Vesuvius erupted and buried the records in A.D. 79, a decision had not yet been given. Now we shall never know whether Justa was freed or reduced to slavery.

Interesting questions remain. Perhaps Telesforus was the unknown father of Justa. Certain phrases he used seemed to hint at this — else why would he have dared to testify against his mistress?

Telesforus was a brave man, and Justa a brave girl. Let us hope they escaped the rising mud which buried the records of Justa's fight for justice.

11 Where Justa was tried

To the law courts in Herculaneum, called the Basilica, came Justa in defence of her rights. The courtroom must have hummed with the whispers of lawyers and clients. The curious spectators must have stared at the pretty young girl, and perhaps they shook their heads disapprovingly at mean Calatoria. Little attention could have been paid to the impressive building itself.

In ancient Greece the *basilikos* was the "King's house." The concept of rule in Rome was transferred to the courts of law, so the courthouse was known as the Basilica. It usually followed a standard design: a rectangular hall rounded at one end (an apse), flanked on each side by a colonnaded aisle. Sometimes galleries for spectators were erected at the sides. The judge sat in a formal toga at the apse end, at a level above everyone else. It is easy to see the similarity between the early Christian churches and the plan of a Roman basilica.

Today the tunnels to the Herculaneum Basilica are heaped with their own rubble and completely closed. They were refilled because the mud cake is less thick at this point, and the houses of Resina above were in danger of collapsing. However, it is still possible to penetrate a little way along one line of massive columns. They remain locked in the mud, some tilted on their bases like toppled ninepins.

The Basilica was not explored and measured carefully, but a rough plan does exist. Its length is great: perhaps sixty metres. While the tunnels remained open, two curious French travellers made their way about the buried law courts with torches. Afterwards they wrote a detailed description of their amazing experience. They reported a long rectangular hall divided by two side rows of columns into a central assembly space. Along

Huge frescoes decorated the Basilica walls. Matching "Hercules and Telephus" was this famous painting of "Chiron and Achilles." The old centaur Chiron is instructing the boy Achilles on the lyre. For his safety, Achilles had been dressed as a girl and hidden among girls. So it was necessary for the centaur to teach Achilles all the manly arts.

the walls, niches held statues. At the rear was a huge statue of the Emperor Vespasian. On either side were large semicircular niches with frescoes.

These paintings eventually were removed and are now among the treasures of the National Archaeological Museum in Naples. One shows the Centaur Chiron (half man, half horse). He is standing with the boy Achilles, who later fought before the walls of Troy and became a Greek

Hercules watches his little son Telephus being suckled by a doe. Telephus was abandoned in a forest by his mother, but saved by the doe and shepherds. This huge colourful fresco was painted in the Herculaneum Basilica, or courthouse. It is considered one of the finest surviving examples of ancient painting.

hero. As a child, Achilles was dressed as a girl and hidden among girls for his safety. When Achilles put off girl's clothing, Chiron became his instructor in all the manly arts. One was music, and the Centaur is teaching Achilles how to play the lyre.

Another fresco illustrates an incident from the life of Hercules. A sun-bronzed Hercules, shown from the rear and wearing only a flower garland and a quiver, stands watching a naked little boy. The boy is being suckled by a doe, while the doe lovingly licks his leg. The boy is Telephus, one of Hercules' many sons. Telephus had been abandoned by his mother in a forest and finally rescued by shepherds.

The third fresco shows the Greek hero Theseus triumphant over the Minotaur, a monster with the body of a man and the head of a bull. Theseus has just stepped out of the labyrinth. Behind him the monster lies dead. The hero is nude except for a purple cloak flung over his left arm. He carries his weapon, his staff, in one hand. Naked youths kneel before him and in the background a worshipful crowd looks on.

Who was the artist? Unfortunately the frescoes are not signed. They are of very great skill and are considered the best examples of ancient painting known to us. If a tiny town like Herculaneum could command such an artist or artists for its courts, what of the great cities? Imagine such paintings in the law courts in *your* town!

The Basilica was artistically remarkable for another reason: on top of the building was the largest bronze four-horse chariot and driver known to us. It probably crowned the entrance. Unluckily it was swept away by the mud. Fragments have been found in several different places. The patient work of reconstruction is like a jigsaw puzzle. One life-size horse is now complete in the Naples Museum. Another head has been recovered. As each new piece appears, the beauty of the whole becomes apparent.

The entrance to the Basilica was flanked by two towering marbles: life-size statues of the Proconsul Marcus Nonius Balbus and his son, Marcus Junior, on horseback. A Proconsul was one of the most powerful of Roman officials, and Herculaneum was proud to be the hometown of such a person. Balbus was the Roman ruler of the island of Crete and portions of North Africa.

Inside the Basilica were the marble portraits of the entire Balbus family, all slightly larger than life. They were found still standing on their pedestals, or fallen nearby. (All are now in the Museum in Naples.) An inscription (now in the Museum, too) states that Balbus rebuilt the Basilica after the earthquake with his own money. The letters are at least thirty centimetres large, chiselled in marble and painted red. A grateful town erected the family statues.

These statues are interesting and important because they are like a photograph album of a leading Roman family. Oddly enough, the name "Balbus" was once a nickname: it meant "stutterer." They were not an old patrician family, but had been wealthy for several generations. The

Life-size bronze horse, one of four from the Basilica — the law courts where Justa was tried. The horses pulled the largest ancient bronze chariot ever discovered. It stood over the entrance pediment to the law courts. Probably the driver was an emperor or a god. The group was toppled and swept away by the mud. Portions continue to be found.

Right: Full-length portrait statue of the Proconsul Marcus Nonius Balbus, head of Herculaneum's most important family. He wears his official toga — an uncomfortable garment Roman men avoided as often as possible. This statue probably stood in the Theatre. The Proconsul died shortly before Vesuvius's eruption in A.D. 97.

Proconsul must have had close connections with the Emperor Vespasian, who was not patrician, but the son of a tax collector.

On their handsome marble horses the Proconsul and his son ride without saddles. They are dressed identically in thigh-length tunics, soft riding shoes, breastplates, swords in scabbards, cloaks thrown over left shoulders and left arms. The left hands hold the reins. On the third finger of each

Above: Marcus Nonius Balbus Junior on horseback. This was one of a marble pair of horses in the Basilica — the other was ridden by the Proconsul. Amazingly, both survived the eruption intact. Marcus Junior wears a cloak flung over his left shoulder, a sword, a breastplate over a short tunic, and soft leather shoes. Note that, like most Romans, he rides bareback. Both statues are now in the Naples Archaeological Museum.

Right: The courtyard, or atrium, of the house that almost certainly belonged to the Balbus family. The white discs are marble "oscilla" carved on both sides. They could be turned at will (oscillate). The columns and walls were painted red. A statue stood in the centre fountain.

left hand is a large signet ring. The right hands are raised aloft in gestures of imperial command. Both faces are cleanshaven (and their legs may have been). The Proconsul's hairline is receding while the son's abundant hair is rather long and combed forward in the Roman fashion.

The other members of the family are shown with the usual Roman realism. The wife, Volasennia, is an average Roman matron and seems bored. Traces of reddish-blonde paint remain on her hair, indicating that she probably used the blonde dye which was popular with Roman women at that time. Or she may have worn a wig — hair once on the head of some barbarian woman.

The two daughters perhaps were called Nonia the Younger and Nonia

Left: Close-up of the Proconsul astride his horse. He and his son are dressed exactly alike. Below left: Close-up of Marcus Junior. His slight frown is puzzling. Was he less comfortable than his father in the role of a powerful administrator? Perhaps he was a little rebellious, too. Or uncertain of himself. Below right: The Proconsul's mother, Viciria. The back of her head was sheared away in the eruption, but has been restored. Full-length portrait statues of all the Balbus women stood in the Basilica.

Below left: The Proconsul's wife Volasennia. She appears as a typical well-to-do matron. Traces of red paint remain on her hair. In life she must have dyed her hair or used a reddish-blonde wig made from the hair of some barbarian women. Below right: The older Balbus daughter, probably called Nonia the Elder. Her statue base with its name inscription has not yet been excavated. She dyed her hair as her mother did. Her figure suggests that she had borne several children. Right: The younger Balbus daughter, probably called Nonia the Younger. Her statue shows no evidence of paint, so she must have left her hair its natural colour.

the Elder, from "Nonius," in accord with old Roman custom. They seem very proper. Their hair has been parted in the middle and brushed back in close-fitting waves to a tight bun on the neck. The elder is a little plump. Slight traces of paint reveal that she may have coloured her hair like her mother. The younger daughter is slim and seems shy, rather withdrawn. Both are plain, but the younger daughter is prettier.

It is the grandmother Viciria, mother of the Proconsul, who is a true masterpiece of Roman portrait art. She towers as an old-fashioned matron — harsh, inflexible, dominating. Her stern, stony features are accented by an oversize nose. Her mouth is firm and her jaw is set. She must have been both pious and rigid in the old Roman religion. She stares down from her pedestal, her heavy body wrapped in a cloak, a hood partly covering her head. Her hair is parted in the middle and brushed severely back. Her strong right hand is raised almost to her chin. The Balbus household no doubt was well managed by grandmother Viciria. It seems unlikely to have been a jolly one.

Written on a wall of the house which probably belonged to Balbus are two proverbs. They are in tiny, regular letters:

"Who does not know how to defend himself, does not know how to survive."

"Even a small danger becomes great if neglected."

Who in that house, other than Marcus Junior, could have written them?

It is amazing that all the members of such a family were discovered. After studying their statues for a while, they almost come to life. It is easy to imagine them at the Theatre, Marcus Junior competing in the sports arena, the Proconsul strutting about the Forum, the mother gossiping at the Baths, the girls shopping, all of them dining in the fountain-splashed courtyard of their luxurious house above the marina.

What a sight, to have been present when this family emerged from the centuries-darkness of the Basilica into the glaring light of day . . . ! Once again they moved through the streets of the town they knew so well. But nobody knows whether or not they escaped.

12 Sports - the arena

The Romans believed that healthy bodies made healthy minds. One of their favourite sayings was, "A sound mind in a sound body." (*Mens sana in corpore sano.*) The Greeks had the same idea. The Greek tradition of the Olympic Games blended in southern Italy with the Roman tradition of sporting events at festivals to stress healthy bodies.

The importance of sports is made clear by the huge size of the sports arena and public gymnasium (Palaestra) in so small a town as Herculaneum. To the Bourbon tunnellers, the Palaestra was bewildering. They thought they had stumbled on a great temple or a vast private villa. The modern visitor can hardly believe what he sees. The arena is larger than the whole of a modern sports ground, containing several football pitches.

Within, a columned enclosed walk surrounded the open sports area on three sides. On the north, or shady side, was a portico and a loggia where officials and special guests watched the competitions. Next to the loggia was a large and beautiful meeting hall which seated hundreds. As yet, only two sides have been completely excavated. In one of the rooms the Bourbon tunnellers scratched their names and the date 1750.

The main entrance to the Palaestra is like the majestic inner portion of a Greek temple. But the tunnellers burrowed through the vault, and when the mud was removed the ceiling collapsed. Other parts are better preserved.

The remaining height of the main hall is about four storeys. A huge niche, now empty, is like a cinema screen at the back of this semicircular hall. In the niche probably stood a heroic statue of Hercules, for he was patron of all sports centres. In front of the niche is a heavy marble table with legs carved as eagle claws. On this table the victors' crowns, made of wreaths cut from a wild olive tree, were placed. It was a Greek custom

Here, in the grand hall of the Palaestra, or public gymnasium, winning athletes were awarded their olive wreaths. The crowns were placed on the big marble table in the centre. Remaining height of the hall is over twelve metres. A colossal statue of Hercules probably stood in the niche. Tunnellers got here before modern excavators and scratched their names and the year (1750) on a wall.

that a well-formed boy, whose parents were living, would cut the wreaths with a golden knife.

Into the main hall marched all the athletes, totally naked and glistening with olive oil on their bronzed skins. They were accompanied by trumpet players. All sought the blessing of Hercules at the beginning of the games. In this hall sacrifices probably were offered, usually kids or lambs.

By the first century A.D., educated Romans no longer placed the slightest faith in such rituals. Nevertheless here stood the priests of Hercules, arms raised and palms held upward. Entrails were inspected to learn if the sacrifice was pleasing to the gods. Mingled smoke from incense and the sacrifice rose before the image of the hero-god. Then the boys and young

Bronze serpent with five heads that spouted water into the Palaestra's cross-shaped swimming pool. The serpent is about twice the height of a man. Here it is photographed in the columned walk or peristyle. Now it has been restored to its original place.

men marched out again, around the whole arena. To the music of flutes the games began.

The sports events were paid for by some wealthy citizen, usually a patrician. The feasts that followed were paid for by rich freedmen. We know that the Proconsul Balbus was one of those who sponsored the Herculaneum games. On the day of Vesuvius' eruption, a stone-toss competition was apparently under way. The excavators found round stones, weighing about two kilogrammes each, laid out for use.

The playing field itself was spacious. There was plenty of room for a row of towering trees, probably umbrella pines, for their roots have been found. The field was large enough for all of the exhibition sports: foot races, wrestling, discus hurling, javelin toss, and a wrestling-boxing combination.

In Herculaneum, as water was plentiful, swimming must have been added. In the centre of the field is a swimming pool in the form of a cross. It is fifty metres long, with a cross arm of thirty metres. At the ends were fountain jets. In the centre is a giant bronze serpent coiled on the limbs of a bronze tree. From the serpent's five crowned heads water sprayed into the pool. It is evident that the Romans tried to make all their public places beautiful. A smaller pool, probably used by the younger competitors, was also beautiful.

The mountain of hard mud has not yet been removed from above the cross-shaped pool. It is merely hollowed out like a cavern over the central portion. To walk the full length of the pool you must go through tunnels. Here you best realize the volume of the volcanic mass and also its force. Carbonized beams, chunks of marble pavement, bits of mosaics, fallen columns — all are scattered as if stirred by some giant's child into an enormous mud pie, then baked until dry and hard.

Only the word "terrifying" can describe this scene. But surely some day the whole sports arena will again be on view. And perhaps games will be held there, as plays are now given in the Pompeii Theatre. Perhaps young athletes from all countries will be represented in a "little league" Olympics at Herculaneum.

13 Fun at the baths

Bathing, for the Romans, was not a chore but like going to a party. The baths were places for cleanliness and fun. Young and old, rich and poor — almost everybody went daily.

Few houses needed private baths. None could compare with the attractions of the public baths. Some were town-owned and some were private enterprises. The public baths were used collectively. Many were more elaborate and better equipped than modern country clubs. The citizens of Herculaneum, like the citizens of Rome, loved the baths. We can only marvel at what they built.

No people in European history have been so clean as the Romans. After Rome fell to the barbarians, bathing came to be despised in the West until modern times. The early Christian dislike of the body had much to do with general indifference to filth. But the body was an object of admiration and respect to the Romans, as to the Greeks. Both kept it clean and produced great sculpture and paintings idealizing it.

Nudity was accepted as a natural state. In early times, bathing was without clothing. Later, women wore a light covering garment while bathing in mixed company, and men wore brief leather loincloths. Later still, mixed bathing was forbidden. In small towns, as at Herculaneum, men and women had separate sections of the baths or different hours. Poor and rich mingled. The well-to-do were accompanied by their slaves.

Almost all baths were equipped with a gymnasium and with courts for ball games. A favourite game was bladder-ball (pila). It was played with inflated animal bladders, often painted green. By the end of the first century A.D., exercise attracted more and more girls and women. They not only played ball, but even went in for fencing. When the exercises

111

were completed, the body was rubbed with olive oil. Then it was scraped with a strigil (strigilis) — a curved instrument of bone or bronze that somewhat resembled a small boomerang. Massages, too, were popular with everyone.

After exercise came the bath. In the waiting-room patrons undressed and waited their turn to go into the warm room (tepidarium) or the hot room (caldarium). From either, they hurried into the cold room (frigidarium) with its cold-water plunge. After the cold plunge they had a quick rub down by attendants. Then they dressed and relaxed in the garden in conversation with friends. They were not content with a fresh-scrubbed smell, so perfume was used by both women and men.

Snacks, eaten with a little wine, were provided for patrons who were hungry. Some baths had "relaxing rooms" for those who wished to hear poetry recited. Some evidently had "relaxing rooms" like private dining-rooms for parties. Many also had libraries and reading-rooms. Every effort was made to decorate the baths as beautifully as possible.

In the cities the baths had arcades or garden paths for strolling among flowers, fountains and music to soothe nerves, and galleries filled with statuary and paintings to charm the eye. So a visit to the baths was cleansing, refreshing, and pleasing to body and spirit.

Even so small a town as Herculaneum had two sets of baths. One was near the centre, now known as the Forum Baths. The other was on the marina outside the walls, now known as the Suburban Baths.

The Forum Baths occupied the southern end of a whole block, with entrances on three different streets. A patron could go direct to the open-air gymnasium if he wished. The main hall has preserved the usual scribbling by people bored with waiting — names in Latin and Greek mingled with doodle drawings. The garden was surrounded by a columned walk. To one side was an open-air exercise and playing area. As this space was not big enough for ball games, a covered "penthouse" court was built on an upper storey.

Of the wall writings in the waiting-room to the woman's section, one was a scrawled salute to the poet Ovid — who wrote *The Art of Love*. Others were a quick sketch of an unclothed girl; several phallic good-luck charms; and the Latin alphabet as far as Q. Perhaps that was the letter on which Vesuvius exploded.

The Forum Baths were about a hundred years old at the time of the eruption. Their plan follows the standard Roman pattern. Off one

The Public Baths, near the Forum, survived the eruption with little damage. Only the plaster is broken off the walls of the men's waiting-room. The seats were originally covered with marble (plundered by tunnellers). The marble floor remains. The round marble basin was for washing hands, the rectangular basin (left) for washing feet before entering the pool. Two skeletons were found on the shelf — persons trapped by the mud.

entrance is a doorkeeper's cubbyhole and the public latrine. The latrine was flushed with water flowing from the cold plunge to avoid waste. In the men's dressing-room a marble bench runs around three sides, and a marble shelf has individual spaces for clothing. The ceiling is vaulted. The pavement is made of irregular pieces of black, grey, and white marble — the inexpensive scrap. The pavement is slightly curved like a bowl to make the floor easier to wash and drain. At one end is a basin of white marble, and in one corner another basin, set lower. The first was used for washing hands, the second for washing feet before entering the other chambers of the Baths. The entire room was lighted (and heated) by a large round window high in the south wall.

In this room two skeletons were found — a man and a woman. Perhaps they worked at the Baths. In any case, they did not flee, thinking they would be safe under the massive thickness of the vault, high on a shelf. They did not expect a river of rising mud. True, the vault remains — and so do they.

The warm, or tepid, room opens off the dressing-room. The floor was hollow for the passage of hot air. It collapsed from the weight of the mud. But as it sank, the mosaic design remained almost undamaged — a huge Triton with legs of curling sea serpents, surrounded by leaping dolphins.

Next to the tepid room is the hot room. Here the vault collapsed, revealing the terra-cotta hot air pipes in the walls. At one end is a huge marble basin, like a birdbath, that contained cold water to wash sweat from the eyes. At the other end was the hot-water plunge.

The cold room with its cold-water plunge was round, with seats in niches for those who wanted to watch. Bronze candelabra prove that the plunge was used at night. The walls are painted dark red, the niches golden yellow. On the blue-grey vault are painted marine creatures: fish, lobster, a moray eel captured by an octopus. When no one was swimming, these were reflected in the water of the green pool below.

The women's section of the Forum Baths is similar to the men's, except that it lacks a cold room and a cold plunge. Clearly the women did not want a frigidarium. They too have a Triton and hot pipes in the walls. But the pipes are thicker than in the men's section. The women liked their water hotter, as is shown by a separate boiler for their unit. It was beside the men's boiler that a long iron poker was found, just where it was dropped when the attendant jumped and ran.

Compared with the standard Forum Baths, the Suburban Baths are very much out of the ordinary. Their position is unusual. They were built outside the town walls overlooking the marina, like an elegant yacht club. Their plan and decorations are unusual, too. In fact, no similar public baths are known to have survived anywhere, so they are one of the great finds of archaeology. Their state of preservation, in spite of exceptional difficulties in digging, is almost incredible.

The entrance courtyard to the Suburban Baths is a terrace. In it stood a statue of the Proconsul Marcus Nonius Balbus (now lost) and a memorial to the Proconsul (still largely intact). The memorial inscription states that Balbus at his own expense restored the Basilica, gates, and walls of the town after the great earthquake. He bore the expense of the youth games and

Tepid room of the women's section of the Public Baths. The shelf compartments were for clothing. Note the complex pattern of the mosaic floor. The women's section had more radiant heat pipes than the men's — they liked their rooms hotter, so a separate furnace unit was necessary.

helped erect a colossal statue of the Emperor Vespasian. As we have seen, an equestrian statue was erected in his honour, and a list of his titles was given. Two words cut in the stone were misspelt — the shift from Latin to Italian had already begun.

From the choice of site for the Proconsul's statue, it seems that he also gave the Suburban Baths to the town. Also his own house appears to have been next door, with connecting ramps. On a ramp wall is scribbled a verse which has nothing to do with the Proconsul. It was written by someone in love:

> *Portumnous loves Amphianda*
> *Januarius loves Veneria*
> *We pray Venus*
> *That you should hold us in mind —*
> *This only we ask you.*

Though the torrent of mud swept away the walls of nearby houses, the snugly placed Suburban Baths lost hardly a stone. But the volcanic mud turned hard as rock, and the water table changed. Because of the hardness of the mud and water seepage, excavations were slow and difficult. They could not be completed until a modern automatic pumping system was installed. Otherwise the present visitor would be sloshing about in a metre or more of water.

The entrance has four massive red columns placed at the corners of a square white marble fountain. The water flows from a bust of the sun god Apollo, a fine Greek sculpture. The Roman valve still works. Light comes from a skylight placed above four rows of arches, showing that the architect was both daring and skilful. All the doors and windows have wide wooden frames, like expensive picture frames in an art gallery.

Two cloakrooms flank each side of the entrance stairway. Here patrons left their clothing — like a cloakroom today for overcoats. The patron, probably wearing a linen wrap or towel, went on to a waiting-room. This room was heated in winter by hot air pipes in the walls, somewhat like modern radiant heat.

The waiting-room was one of the most exciting finds ever made by archaeologists. It is exactly as it was two thousand years ago, except that the Bourbon tunnellers destroyed the decorations of the vaulted ceiling. Luckily they got no deeper.

Light enters through a glass-enclosed window in a ceiling niche. The pavement is made of black marble squares separated by white marble bands. Three walls have white marble benches set against many-coloured marble backgrounds. But it is naked warriors formed in stucco that make this room so remarkable. The warriors, about seventy centimetres high in framed panels, are the work of some first-class artist and were hardly damaged by the eruption. Nor were the wooden doors carbonized. They are handsomely panelled, as if for a palace. They remain on their original hinges in their original places.

The tepid room is also amazing. The walls are covered with paintings of fantastic architecture, as if in a dream. They are heated with inset terra-cotta tubes. The swimming pool, too, is heated. To one side is a small round sweat room with seats in niches, like a modern sauna. It is as finely decorated as a jewel cabinet.

The hot room has the usual marble pool for hot water and the usual round marble basin for cold water. Here the force of the mud is dramatically

The Suburban Baths are the most complete ever discovered anywhere. They were built on the marina near the Balbus house and probably were the Proconsul's gift to the town. Here is the entrance foyer during excavation. The hardened mud is being chipped away from the fountain of Apollo. Today water spurts from the original pipes. The columns were painted red.

117

Stucco warrior on the wall of the waiting-room of the Suburban Baths. Such stucco decorations are very fragile, thus very rare. Several warriors are in different poses. All carry the standard equipment of Greek warriors: spear, sword, shield, helmet, cloak for cool nights. Occasionally shin guards were added.

illustrated. The steaming mix flowed in through the window and over-turned the massive marble basin. Then the mud pushed the basin across the room and left it stranded, balanced on edge.

The plunge in the cold room is lined with red marble, with white marble steps, and a white marble bottom. Quite a fancy swimming pool, anywhere, anytime. Not many people have had a chance to swim in anything like it today.

The lounge was used for relaxing conversation over a snack and a glass of wine. It had two large picture windows overlooking the sea and a third overlooking the marina. The furniture was probably wicker chairs set beside small round tables. The decorations were handsome, though now badly damaged.

The Suburban Baths offer additional surprises. The furnace room is complete with its pipes, boiler, and wood still stacked on the floor. Water was piped from the town aqueduct. In one room is a heap of hollow bricks, unbroken. They were being used in repairs. In the back corridor the wooden scaffolding is still stacked against the wall, uncarbonized. Also unscorched are wooden shutters. Thirty-five roof tiles are stamped with the name of the manufacturer: M(arcus) AC(cius) AMP(liatus).

At the end of the corridor was a private dining or party room. Jokers drew caricatures of two friends on the wall. The lady is shown with her nose comically prolonged, wearing a crown of vine leaves. The gentleman is shown with an absurdly receding chin, wearing an affected, high-combed, curled hairdo.

These white walls seem to have been as tempting as a modern black-board. A slave left this record of his visit: "I, Hermeros, slave of my mistress Primagenia, came from Puteoli to Timnianus Street and am looking for the bank messenger, the slave of Phoebus."

Another graffito relates: "Two companions were here. After the bad guidance of Epaphroditus in everything, they tardily threw him out. Then with the girls they joyfully consumed $105\frac{1}{2}$ sesterces." Sesterces were one unit of Roman money. A fairly expensive party, it may be said.

Other graffiti are gay and bawdy — probably scrawled by persons who were drinking wine. Certainly the Suburban Baths were a lively place from any point of view.

14 Entertainments

Ancient Romans would feel perfectly at home in the modern theatre. Roman drama and the Roman theatre are the direct ancestors of our own. In *The Boys From Syracuse* and *A Funny Thing Happened on the Way to the Forum* and other plays and films, we have seen and laughed at Roman comedy. At Herculaneum both the Theatre itself and the performance would have seemed familiar to us. Some things would have struck us with their novelty.

The Herculaneum Theatre is the one ancient theatre thus far discovered intact. The mud rose higher and higher on the outside until it flowed over the upper edge as into an open bowl. The mud swept away only the statuary around the edges. All else was preserved.

Unfortunately for us the Theatre was plundered for many years. We have seen how princes and kings used it as merely a source of precious marbles, statuary, and jewels. For almost forty years the tunnelling in and out of the Theatre went on, despite the fact that it lay buried under thirty metres of hardened mud. Modern archaeologists say that in less time, and probably at no greater cost, the whole structure could have been uncovered. If it had been revealed and not plundered, it would be today one of the archaeological wonders of the world.

Revealed would have been an important Greek-Roman theatre at the moment of rehearsal for an afternoon performance. Theatrical shows were usually part of festivals. The old Greek dramas as well as Roman products were favoured by the Greek-speaking people of southern Italy. Because Herculaneum was close to Neapolis, it probably attracted the best troupes of actors from Athens, Alexandria (the famed Greek city in Egypt), and Rome.

120

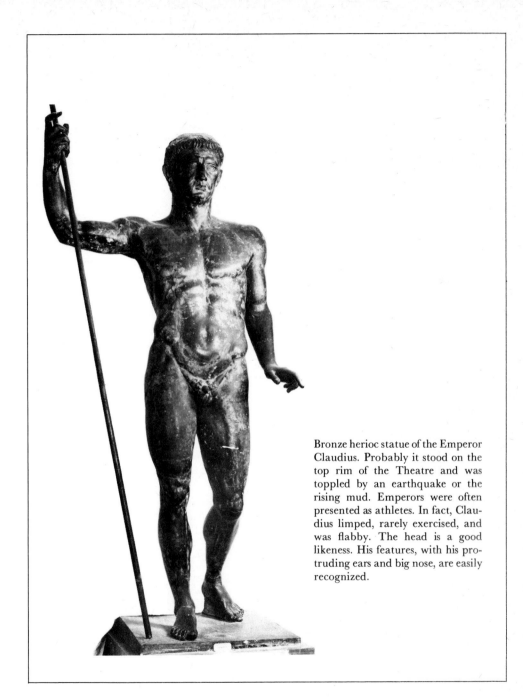

Bronze herioc statue of the Emperor Claudius. Probably it stood on the top rim of the Theatre and was toppled by an earthquake or the rising mud. Emperors were often presented as athletes. In fact, Claudius limped, rarely exercised, and was flabby. The head is a good likeness. His features, with his protruding ears and big nose, are easily recognized.

Like tragedy, comedy and farce were in great demand. Except for gladiatorial combats and chariot races, pantomimes were the most popular of all spectacles. Little or no spoken dialogue was used in the pantomimes. Singing and dancing were the important parts.

In the old Roman theatre, all roles had been played by men. By the time of the Empire, actresses had come into their own, especially in the pantomimes. Masks, tragic and comic, had been worn by all actors. They were dropped, and actors faced the audience just as actors do today. Successful actors became idolised like film stars today. They commanded big money and fashionable friends — sometimes emperors and empresses. All the same, laws continued to discriminate against actors, and they were set apart from the rest of the population.

By the year of Vesuvius' eruption, the pantomime had become very similar to modern musical comedy. The leading actors and actresses were singing and dancing stars. Costumes were often scanty, especially for chorus girls. For some parts, nothing at all was worn. A male role such as Apollo was played without costume, as was Venus and other goddesses. In the satyr plays, actors wore goatskin loincloths, leather phalli, and goat tails. Essential in all comedy was the double-meaning joke and gesture, which drew laughter from the noisy and disrespectful audiences.

Imagine the Herculaneum Theatre on the day of Vesuvius' explosion: yellow and blue awnings slung from masts across the whole structure to protect the audience from the sun; many-coloured seat cushions on the stone seats; attendants spraying saffron-scented water from skin bottles to freshen the heavy air; salesmen hawking trays of sweets and nuts; people quarrelling over tickets; children examining the curtain, with its machinery for *descending* into the pit; the trapdoors on the stage; the creaky cranes for flying the gods through space; the huge bronze drums for making thunder; the revolving scenery; the many musical instruments; the costumes, with masks, wigs, high-heeled shoes for tragic actors and low-heeled shoes for comic actors; paint, powder, and other make-up; and finally, pages and pages of scripts.

The Herculaneum Theatre is considered an architectural jewel. It seated twenty-five hundred people. After the fall of Rome, such theatres as this were not to be seen again until the sixteenth century. The Herculaneum Theatre had been built in the time of the Emperor Augustus. It was not cut into a hillside, as in Greece or in Pompeii, but stood independently like the theatres of Neapolis and Rome. It was, however, a

Small framed painting found at Herculaneum called the "Player King." An actor is dressed for his royal role. The kneeling woman writes under a theatrical mask, while a man in the background changes costume. The scene is backstage, or the actors would be wearing masks. This is one of the most famous paintings surviving from ancient times. The colours are delicate and skilfully applied.

semicircle supported by arches and pillars. All the decorations were very rich.

It was the stage that displayed the true pomp of the building. The stage had a permanent architectural background of rare marbles and statuary. Walls and columns were faced with marbles of black, yellow, purple, and

Left: Among the most recent small find was a flute. Note the mouthpiece. Other instruments played at the theatre and elsewhere were the trumpet, pipes, zither, lyre, drums, and cymbals. Musical comedies, called "pantomimes," required a full orchestra. Flute music was enjoyed during meals.

Right: Odd objects that may be theatre tickets, but no one is sure. Roman numerals may indicate seating sections. Tickets were free. The fish is carved of expensive ivory, so it could have been issued only to an important person.

red. Some were faced with alabaster. A second curtain, as in other Roman theatres, must often have been raised in front, so that painted scenery could be used. The Romans always liked realism in theatrical settings.

Above the orchestra, stone seats filled the auditorium (cavea) in semi-circular tiers. Flights of steps led to the various seat groupings. The first four rows were reserved for local magistrates, officials from Rome, and distinguished citizens. The next sixteen rows were reserved for aristocrats. The remainder of the seats were separated by a barrier about a metre high. Here sat ordinary citizens, including women and children.

The highest officials sat in boxes over entrances to the orchestra, at either end of the stage. No doubt one was reserved for the Proconsul Balbus and his family, for his rank was far above that of any local magistrate. In Greek theatres, unlike the Roman, seats were not reserved on a class basis. In Roman theatres all seats were free, and only slaves were barred.

Theatre exits (at Herculaneum, there were seven) were called "vomitoria" for obvious reasons. Now it is the sport of guards at Herculaneum and Pompeii to have a little joke with visiting tourists. They tell the gullible that the Romans gorged themselves at meals, then vomited to eat more. Then they point to various open holes in private houses as "vomitoria"! A good example of the way misinformation gets started and is believed.

Today the original Theatre tunnels and the monks' well remain much as they were when the explorations were abandoned. Here the visitor receives a vivid impression of the working conditions of the Neapolitan diggers deep underground. Mists and vapours slither like ghosts through the corridors. Water and slime drip from the ceilings and walls. The air is dank, bone-chilling. Squeaking bats dart from the darkness. Even with electric lights the tunnels disappear abruptly into the mysterious tomb-like darkness of twenty centuries. The imprint of a statue's face in the hardened mud seems a demonic leer. Echoes re-echo, like screams of a crowd in panic.

All this some day will change, when complete excavation again opens the Theatre to a living audience and the excitement of the greatest plays of antiquity.

15 The main street

Romans, as great organisers, considered a town without a Forum not a town at all. The Forum was the centre of civic life, of banking, of trade. The Forum was a place for people to meet and talk about business and politics, and also gossip.

In spite of the maze of tunnels and shafts, early information gained about the Herculaneum Forum was scanty. Yet a town with public buildings as impressive as the Palaestra, Basilica, and Baths was sure to have an impressive Forum.

When the main street was discovered, it was clear that the Forum could not be far away. The old eighteenth-century map (drawn on the basis of the tunnels) showed a main street and an open area that might have been the Forum. But the map was not exact. Worse, both the main street and the Forum appeared to be under one of the most congested Resina slums. So before the dig, houses had to be torn down. It has been a slow and costly process. Only part of the main street has been uncovered. The Forum is yet to come.

Compared with the other narrow streets of Herculaneum, the main street is very wide — about thirteen metres. Included are pavements of three or four metres on each side. The street was a pedestrian paradise, as carts, wagons, chariots were banned from the area. (In Rome, all wheeled traffic was banned except at night. Chariots were banned except during a Triumph.) Stone steps or stone pillars blocked the Herculaneum main street to vehicles.

The kerbstones are low and the gutters are of brick. The paving is of smooth stones. The pavement on the southern side was protected by overhanging roofs, some of which were supported by carved wooden beams still to be seen. On the north a covered path with columns protected shoppers from rainy weather. Here was found the partially open carton of fine glassware. But solid mud still fills the house or shop.

The main street begins with a little square in front of the assembly hall of the sports arena. It is marked by a public fountain. A jet of water spurts from a crudely carved head of Hercules into a rectangular trough. Farther down the street is another fountain, this with an image of Venus. Nearby is a painted shrine with serpents. At intervals smaller streets lead down towards the seafront. Town notice "boards" were placed at these intersections. One, a stone pillar, carries a town ordinance against dropping litter. The penalty was a fine or a whipping, or both.

A continuous line of shops and workshops opened on both sides of the street. Mixed in was an occasional patrician house. One typical workshop was the tinker's, where a bronze statuette of Bacchus is still waiting for repair. Another was an artist's shop, where a panel of cupids was being painted.

Advertising here is more restrained than in Pompeii, where merchants and politicians went in for the hard sell. In Herculaneum a typical advertisement is a painting of Bacchus on the wall of a wine shop. A half-dozen samples of various types of wine are shown. The clear meaning is that these wines are fit for a god. The slogan is short and modern: COME TO THE SIGN OF THE WINE BOWLS! (Romans drank wine from bowls.)

The old map indicates that a great temple is to be found at the end of the main street. If so, the temple remains far distant. At the end of the short section already excavated, a massive four-way arch dominates the street. Originally it was faced with marble and decorated with stuccoes. As only traces remain, evidently the Bourbons got here first. When they arrived, the arch had four equestrian bronzes. We know this from remaining fragments of the horses' feet. It was an imposing arch, similar to those in ancient Rome.

Across the street is one of the structures most recently excavated: the "Shrine of the Augustales." This shrine was the headquarters of the Augustales, the officials responsible for worship of the deified emperors. This worship served a definite political purpose. It attempted to establish a single unifying religion — like the universal Latin language — among all the different peoples of the Roman Empire.

The Augustales were established in A.D. 14 by a decree of the Senate deifying the dead Emperor Augustus. Following emperors were so powerful, so glorified, and so elevated that it was easy for distant peoples to accept the Caesar as a god. The emperors had assumed the title "Pontifex Maximus," or High Priest of the Roman religion. So deification was but one more step. (The Roman Catholic Pope carries the same title today.)

In Herculaneum the Augustales headquarters has an inscription stating that the first banquet was given by "Proculus and Julian." That banquet might have been something like a modern stag party. Roman men did not like to be sombre at meals. The tunnellers stripped the hall of almost everything except the inscription.

At the back is an arched niche which held a statue of a deified Emperor, probably Vespasian. He died only a month before the eruption. As death approached, he moaned, "Alas! I must be turning into a god . . . !" It was his last joke.

The Augustales have left us a mystery. One portion of the hall was closed off by a temporary partition (the "trellis work" we have seen). This formed a small room that had but one door and one tiny barred window. The window looked inward into the hall. In the room are only two pieces of furniture: a bed and a table. Both are of wood and of fine quality.

On the bed is the skeleton of a man. He seems to have thrown himself face down — hopelessly waiting for the final surge of rising mud. Who was this man? Why did he fail to escape?

It seems clear that he did not escape because no one unlocked the door. Was he a political prisoner? Was he an important man — too important to occupy an ordinary jail? Was he kept under lock and key by members of his own class?

Vespasian had avoided the bloodletting which had occurred under the Emperor Nero — stabbings, secret executions, forced suicides by vein slashing. But banishment, house arrest, and forced changes of residence had continued. Perhaps an erring member of the Augustales in Rome had been sent to the Augustales in Herculaneum "for his own protection." He might even have been given the run of the town. Or he might have been locked up in a place of luxury.

This sort of thing had happened before in the town of Hercules. Agrippina, the granddaughter of the Emperor Augustus and step-granddaughter of his wife the Empress Livia, was banished to Herculaneum. Agrippina was an obstacle to Livia's schemes to put her own son Tiberius on the throne. After Augustus' death, Agrippina was murdered on Livia's orders.

Recently excavated shrine of the Emperor Augustus, who was deified after his death. The objective was to give a common deity to many different peoples in the Roman Empire. The wall painting shows Hercules with Juno and Minerva. In a locked room off this shrine, the skeleton of a man was found face down on a bed. The skeleton is still there.

Whatever the offence of the man in the barred room, he too paid with his life. Perhaps some day a chance reference will provide the key to that strange little room — and its prisoner who has lain in a position of despair for almost two thousand years.

16 Treasure-troves from the past

While wandering through the streets and buildings of Herculaneum we have seen so great a treasure that it is hard to believe. Yet the most precious objects have not been left in the ancient town. They have been taken away from their original sites and placed under lock and key in museums.

One of these museums is in Herculaneum itself. It is an ordinary Herculaneum house, called the "Antiquarium." The other museum is in Naples and has been mentioned many times in this book. It is the National Archaeological Museum (Museo Nazionale Archeologico). It was built about four hundred years ago as a huge riding school for the aristocracy. Today it houses the world's most important collection from antiquity. These museums, plus the Antiquarium at Pompeii, are true treasure-troves.

In Herculaneum's little museum you can see samples of some of the most valuable bronze and marble statuary, mosaics, and frescoes. But chiefly displayed are hundreds of small things. Here is a random list: combs, mirrors, needles, earrings, beads of amber and glass, candelabra, oil lamps, a lantern of bronze and glass, double-pronged instruments for mending fishing nets, wheat, beans, eggs, pistachio nuts, rope, baskets, part of the counterpane of a bed, fishing net, hinges, a bronze water valve, ink bottles, silver dishes, fish hooks, a carpenter's plane, a heap of nails, money, glass jars, seals, a surveyor's triangle, kitchen pots, wax tablets, amulets, flutes, brooches, rings of all sorts, perfume flasks, pins, a chariot wheel, spoons, weights, scales, medical instruments, and — of all things — a bowl of biscuits (carbonized) baked with a flower pattern. A similar list made in the Naples Museum would seem endless.

The exact sources of many of these objects are unknown. Most were

Lamps were made of bronze or clay and burned olive oil. Sometimes they were decorated with sculpture, like these two similar bronze hand lamps. The one on the left was found at Pompeii, the one on the right at Herculaneum.

found during the period of haphazard tunnelling. It is a pity not to know accurately where a surveyor's triangle was found, or medical instruments, or some of the exceptional jewellery. (Imagine, as one example, a brooch so delicately carved that it compresses a whole Egyptian scene into a space smaller than a fingernail.)

Small objects can be well displayed in museum cases, but furniture, frescoes, mosaics, and statuary do not succeed so well. Usually they were designed in relation to architecture — houses, temples, shops — not the blank rooms of a museum. Objects of art in a museum compete with one another in a way not intended by the artists. The cold light from skylights or neon tubes in enormous dead-white chambers was not intended for a marble Apollo or Venus. So it becomes harder to visualize the god or

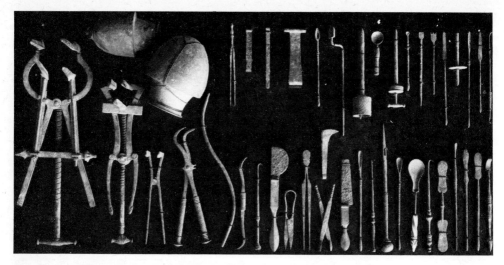

Doctors in ancient times were considered skilled craftsmen. Medical instruments from Pompeii (shown here) and Herculaneum prove the advanced state of Roman surgery. Instruments are specialised for various parts of the body, including brain surgery. Note the similarity to many modern medical and dental instruments.

Below: Wooden tokens carved like a sow with Roman numerals on the underside. Was this a guessing game? Or a raffle? Archaeologists don't know. Numerals found thus far go up to 11 (XI, top).

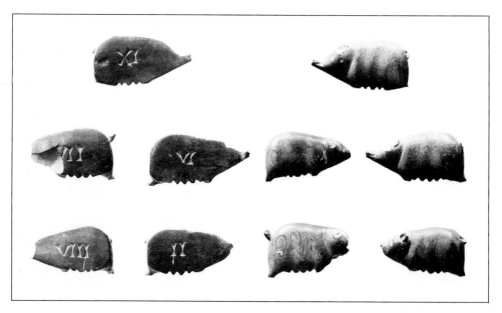

Gladiator's bronze parade helmet discovered at Herculaneum. It is a work of art, decorated with scenes from the Trojan War.

goddess in their original soft and glowing colours, set in a temple of brilliant reds, blues, and golds. What we see today is only a pale grey likeness of the original, often dusty at that. Of course, bronze statuary fares better. But without the original setting, much is lost.

As for the intricate mosaic floors that have been carried away and reset in museums, visitors walk over them with hardly a glance. So the mosaicist's art is not fully appreciated. The same point is true for wall paintings. They were created for individual rooms, and not meant to be lined up beside one another.

If the statuary, frescoes, mosaics, marble pavements, furniture, and personal objects must be taken from an ancient room to a modern museum, then why not move the room itself? Why not keep everything together as it was found? Or why not the whole house?

The best solution, of course, is the ideal of the modern excavators: to leave every object, as far as possible, where it belongs. In this way the excavation site itself becomes the museum — a living scene from a dead past. That past is our own. We can immediately identify and understand.

Lately, excavation at Herculaneum has almost stopped. The present Italian government no longer provides funds for regular exploration. The officials say that Italy has many archaeological sites — which it has — and to provide for them all is too costly. Funds are given for limited maintenance, such as repairs when roofs collapse. Clearly, houses as old as those in the town of Hercules require more than normal attention.

Young volunteers digging at Herculaneum. Students from many countries assemble every summer to help uncover archaeology's treasure-trove. They also polish mosaics, help assemble broken frescoes (like jigsaw puzzles), and sometimes read Latin inscriptions.

Left: Difficulties of the excavation are clearly shown at the entrance to the Forum. The slums of Resina tower above. Diggers must take care that walls and arches do not collapse on them. Note the truck removing rubble. In the centre foreground is a drinking fountain. Its water will flow again some day — if enough money is provided.

So, without funds it has not been possible to train and keep a crew of skilled diggers. Instead, private excavating firms have been called in for short-term jobs. Their methods and workmen are not well-suited to archaeology, as everyone admits.

Another excavation force, a volunteer group, does exist. The "Herculaneum Academy" each summer draws together archaeological students from many countries. They live in a villa not far from the dig. They volunteer their services with pick and shovel. Boys and girls toil steadily under the blistering sun, pitting their muscles against Vesuvius. It is a cheering sight. They take their responsibility to history seriously.

The excavation of Pompeii is nearly completed, while the excavation of Herculaneum is just begun. Only four blocks have been completely uncovered. How many more are there? Of the important public buildings, only the Forum Baths are now entirely visible. Some rooms of the Suburban Baths are not yet cleared, and much of the Palaestra is hidden. The Basilica and the Theatre are totally buried. And other villas like the Villa of the Papyri undoubtedly exist. So, of the whole face of Herculaneum we have seen only the chin.

In future digging, will a small covered theatre for poetry reading (like the one in Pompeii) come to light? Did an amphitheatre exist? What of the covered market, for fish and meat? What of the docks? What of night clubs and taverns? What of the cemetery? And the temples, which surely must be impressive? What of future paintings, statuary, tools, and — perhaps most precious of all — libraries? And how many more graffiti — those personal messages from the past — scribbled on walls? Who can forget the schoolboy who painfully wrote out one of his daily lessons in its entirety? Or the girl who printed: HYACINTHUS WAS HERE. HIS VIRGINIA SALUTES HIM.

Early in our century the English archaeologist Sir Charles Walston said: "Herculaneum is the one site above all others which ought to be excavated." Very recently the American archaeologist Dr. Frank E. Brown added: "Herculaneum is probably archaeology's most flagrant unfinished business." Both were right. Nowhere else do we know of such a time capsule waiting to be opened.

If you found a buried treasure-trove, wouldn't you dig all of it up?

17 Treasure-troves in Britain

Many archaeological sites in Britain suffer through lack of money or the time available to explore them fully. There are still numerous undiscovered remains. Sometimes housing development, a motorway route or a new by-pass will reveal a site, and an archaeologist may be called in to "dig" and survey it. Time may be short — building the houses cannot be delayed or the motorway must stride forward. When this happens an organisation called "Rescue" may come to the site. The archaeologists and volunteers of Rescue will excavate and record all they can before the new buildings or roads either destroy or recover the remains.

On other sites, steady progress can be made, year after year and the picture slowly built up of what was there and what it looked like. You may visit a site and see people at work, carefully uncovering new areas, photographing, surveying, analysing things they have found and so on. Archaeology never reaches a conclusion. There is always something new to be discovered and examined. But it is an expert's subject. You have read how indiscriminate treasure-hunters could have wrecked for ever some parts of Herculaneum. If you are interested in helping on a "dig", join your local society and learn how to excavate properly. Another way is to join Young Rescue, and their address is given at the end of the Reading list.

Above all, visit as many sites as you can. Use your own eyes and discover all you can for yourself. History can be a deadly boring subject, but when places like Herculaneum are discovered, it can be one of the most fascinating and rewarding ways of learning.

Roman Sites in Britain

Many people think Roman Britain as just long straight roads and Hadrian's Wall. But there is much more being discovered each year by archaeologists and historians. It is unlikely that anything quite like Herculaneum will ever be revealed. Wherever you live or go on holiday however, there is probably a Roman site worth visiting. Here are just a few of the many places you could study. (Often the Roman place-name is put on signposts so these have been added in *italics* after the name used now).

Villas

It is important to realise that villas in Britain were very different from the suburban Herculaneum villa described in Chapter 8. Although towns show most clearly the influence of the Romans, the countryside was changed by their coming too. A country villa could be owned by a rich Roman town-dweller or a noble family who had ruled the local tribe before the Roman invasion and was given the villa perhaps as a reward for his co-operation.

The villa was really the centre of a farming estate. It was self-contained and attached to it were workshops for making tools and pottery, stables, quarters for tenants and slaves. British villas vary in size and importance. The early examples were low half-timbered buildings set on stone foundations. The largest villas were often shaped like an E without the middle cross piece. They had two storeys, and were really luxurious ranches. Excavations in the past fifteen years have revealed a super-villa at Fishbourne. It is so grand that it has been called a palace.

Examples: Chedworth, near Cirencester (Gloucestershire)
Lullingstone (Kent)
Bignor (Sussex)
Fishbourne (Sussex)

Baths

As you have seen in Chapter 13, baths were not just places for bathing but were also centres for relaxing, chatting and playing dice and other board games. In Britain there were two types. The spa type like the one at Bath or Buxton is the first. Here the baths were large and you could actually dive in and swim. The second (and most common) type is found throughout the Roman Empire attached to most towns, villas and forts, and can be subdivided into:

(a) Dry heat (like a modern Sauna Bath) and
(b) damp heat (the modern Turkish Bath).

There are several books which explain the central heating systems used in the baths and the various rooms of different temperatures through which the bathers progressed. Often a bath-house can give clues to the size of the town or fort which it served. Here are places where Roman baths can still be seen:

Bath	(Somerset)	*Aquae Sulis*
Chesters	(Northumberland)	*Cilurnum*
Wall	(Staffordshire)	*Letocetum*
Wroxeter	(Shropshire)	*Viriconium*
Chedworth	(Gloucestershire)	

Theatres

The Herculaneum theatre, like those built in this country, followed the Greek pattern fairly closely. A semi-circular pit (called the orchestra) was on front of a raised stage. The audience sat on a sloping semi-circle of seats. Theatres are known to have been built at Brough-on-Humber (Yorkshire) *Petuaria*, Colchester (Essex) *Camulodunum*, and at Canterbury (Kent) *Durovernum*. But only the theatre at St. Albans (Hertfordshire) *Verulanium* is visible today.

Amphitheatres

Many of the towns and forts in Roman Britain had amphitheatres which were the scene of fights between gladiators and of battles between men and wild beasts. Some amphitheatres were large enough to hold a complete legion (about 6,000 men).
Best examples:

Caerleon	(Monmouthshire)	*Isca*
Cirencester	(Gloucestershire)	*Corinium*
Silchester	(Hampshire)	*Calleva*
Dorchester	(Dorset)	*Durnovaria*

Books to read
There are quite a lot of books on Roman Britain. Here is a short list which you may find useful.

Life in Roman Britain by Anthony Birley
Batsford 1964.

Your Book of Roman Britain by David Jones
Faber and Faber 1973.

Boudiccas Revolt by Ian Andrews
Cambridge University Press 1972.

Roman Britain by I. A. Richmond
Penguin 1970.

Young Rescue,
Museum of Archaeology,
Downing Street,
Cambridge.

Index